Celebrations From a Cowgirl's Kitchen

By (

GREAT TEXAS LINE

Celebrations From a Cowgirl's Kitchen

Editor: Amy Culbertson
Cover photo: Ralph Lauer
Cover design: Kari Crane
Book design and layout: Tom Johanningmeier

© Copyright: Great Texas Line Press. All rights reserved. No portion of this book may be reproduced in any form without the written permission of the publisher.

For bulk sales and wholesale inquiries contact:

Great Texas Line Press
Post Office Box 11105, Fort Worth TX 76110
greattexas@hotmail.com
www.greattexasline.com
817-922-8929

To see our complete list of Texas cookbooks, travel guides, sports and humor books, visit greattexasline.com.

Great Texas Line Press strives to be socially responsible, donating a portion of proceeds from several books to Texas nonprofit and cultural organizations while donating hundreds of books annually to National Public Radio stations around the state. Every effort is made to engage Texas writers, editors, illustrators, designers and photographers who have fallen victim to the newspaper industry crisis.

CONTENTS

INTRODUCTION

Cowgirl is an attitude, really; a pioneer spirit, a special American brand of courage. The cowgirl faces life head on, lives by her own lights and makes no excuses. Cowgirls take stands. They speak up. They defend the things they hold dear. A cowgirl might be a rancher, or a barrel racer, or a bull rider, or an actress. But she's just as likely to be a checker at the local Winn Dixie, a full-time mother, a banker, an attorney, or an astronaut. – Dale Evans

Every Texas woman has a little bit of cowgirl in her heart. From the Louisiana border to the western tip of El Paso, you'll encounter every kind of Texas cowgirl. Some herd cattle; some tend to the farm. You'll find city slickers who occasionally break out the cowgirl gear and socialites who wear their boots with a sundress and silver bling; Gulf Coast cowgirls as handy with a fishing rod as with a lariat and caballeras with a Latin flair in the valley of the Rio Grande.

If you love the heritage and hospitality of Texas and embrace the pioneer attitude of the Lone Star State, you can call yourself a Texas cowgirl. And there are as many ways to show your cowgirl style when entertaining as there are ways to express your cowgirl spirit.

In Texas, there's always a reason to celebrate, and you can rely on a resourceful cowgirl to be a generous host. She knows how to entertain for any occasion – from a Sunday church supper to a garden brunch, a cattleman's cocktail party or festive farm-to-table dinner. You can throw any ingredient or scenario at a Texas cowgirl and she'll wrangle up some ideas that will delight any partygoer.

That's how we do it in Texas. The atmosphere is comfortable. The food is seasonal. The recipes have big flavors, and the décor has a style of its own. The spread might include deviled eggs on vintage china, Mason jars filled with iced tea and cheesy casseroles in circa-1970 Pyrex. You'll find cobbler cooked in a cast-iron Dutch oven, enchiladas on Fiestaware and mismatched pieces of Grandma's silver serving up barbecue and creamed corn. It's Texas style, and it never goes out of fashion.

So here you will find everything you need to know about entertaining like a true Texas cowgirl. This book is full of party themes, menus, recipes and décor, along with advice from a Texas cowgirl who's learned to entertain with confidence, ease and style. I may have fallen off the horse a few times, but in true cowgirl style, you get up, dust yourself off with a smile and pass the pecan pie. So pour yourself some iced tea, sit for a spell and let me show you the ropes.

— *Christine Gardner*

CHAPTER 1
COWGIRL ENTERTAINING
WITH EASE AND STYLE

Looking back over the years, I realize I learned to cook so that I could entertain. As a young adult, I found myself filling my weekends with dinner parties, celebrations, gatherings with friends. Soon, all this cooking and entertaining led to a career in catering and special events. Now, ideas for recipes and entertaining fill my every waking moment.

Many people doubt their ability to pull off a simple party. Trust me, you can handle it. In my early years of hosting, I quickly learned there are four important rules to successful entertaining: From a casual dinner party for four to a cocktail party for 50, you must plan ahead, make ahead, have fun and make your guests feel at home.

That final rule is the most important. And if you were raised in Texas, a place where hospitality is as big as the state, you already have an upper hand. I didn't become fully aware of this simple truth until I lived outside Texas. That's where I learned the difference.

This book is filled with ways to cook, entertain and set a table with Texas cowgirl style. Each chapter features a different party theme and a menu tailored to the occasion. Many of the recipes are inspired by Texas classics but updated to reflect contemporary trends and tastes. The themes range from casual – fish fry, fiesta, farm-to-table – to elegant – a vintage bridal shower, a cattleman's cocktail party, a rhinestone-cowgirl barbecue.

Whatever the occasion, entertaining does not need to be complicated. But my years of riding herd on celebrations from simple to splashy have taught me some general guidelines to pulling off the kind of fun and easy soirees that typify the cowgirl way of hosting:

• Plan ahead, starting with lists of the items you'll need for décor and of the recipe ingredients you'll need to pull out of the pantry or purchase. Go through your china cabinet, serving ware, linens and flower vessels: You may find something you'd forgotten about that could be an inspiration for the tablescape or color scheme. Clean, polish or dust each item and gather all your pieces together so they're ready to use.

• Jot down a timeline of what can be prepped or made ahead, so you can do as much as possible before guests arrive. Many of my featured recipes can be made entirely or partially in advance, and for those that can, I've included do-ahead suggestions.

• Be aware of your own limitations. Invite only as many guests as you can handle as the hostess and cook.

• Plan a menu that fits the theme, your guests, the venue, the time you'll have available to prepare and your own cooking ability. It's never a good idea to cook a recipe for the first time for guests; always test the recipe in advance and be sure you like the flavor and understand the technique and timing of the dish.

• Don't stress over details that might be inconsequential to the success of the party. When making your to-do list, prioritize the items on it. Guests may not notice that the napkins aren't ironed, but they will notice if you don't have enough ice or the white wine isn't cold enough.

• Pay particular attention to what will make your guests comfortable. Do you have enough seating? Is the bathroom clean? Have you chosen appropriate background music? (No one likes to walk into a silent room, but few enjoy being bombarded by a booming bass track while mingling or dining.) I've found that overplanning is better than underplanning. I would rather have too much of something than not enough; you can always send people home with leftovers or enjoy the extra bottles of wine at a later date.

• Enlist help for the event, if you need it, so you are free to welcome guests, make people feel at home and keep an eye on details. If you need to man the grill, shake cocktails or check on things in the oven, try to arrange the mingling area close to the grill, bar or kitchen. This way, you can chat with guests and still attend to cooking tasks.

• You want to be completely ready at least 30 minutes before your party's stated start time. Without fail, there is always someone who is early, and it'll be awkward for both you and the early guests if you're still scurrying around trying to get ready.

Proper planning and advance preparation not only will allow you to enjoy your own party but, most importantly, will ensure that your guests have a great time. And remember: This is your party. Use the menus and ideas in the chapters ahead as inspiration, but be sure to weave your own style, family traditions and creativity into each event.

Party themes aside, these are recipes that will be welcome on your table anytime. Each is a tried-and-true favorite that has passed the test of family, friends and party guests. I chose them from my extensive collection because they're crowd-pleasers that meet the cowgirl criteria – with ingredients, flavor and style true to Texas traditions, from the Panhandle to the Valley and from the Piney Woods to the Big Bend.

CHAPTER 2
A VINTAGE BRIDAL BRUNCH

MENU

*Mimosa Bar • Classic Deviled Eggs • Blueberry Blue-Corn Muffins •
Baked Mexican Frittata With Hash-Brown Crust • Wildflower Honey
Granola Parfait • Strawberry Chess Squares*

In Texas, wedding showers, brunches, luncheons and rehearsal dinners
are almost as big a deal as the actual wedding. No one can be left off
the list: family members, friends, neighbors, co-workers, acquaintances
— and don't forget your mom's second cousin whom you haven't seen
since you were in first grade.

As the guest list grows, then, the menu, decor and preparation need to
be simple but impressive. So think vintage, rustic, country charm.

Vintage style doesn't mean you can't mix new with old, or rustic with
elegant. Don't be afraid to pair vintage china with modern pieces. Look
around your home or borrow from a friend, gathering antique dishes,
decorative pieces, artwork, linens and creative vessels for flowers, food
and candles.

At an East Texas event I catered last year, the hostess topped long
tables with lace tablecloths, simple white napkins and dinner plates
holding antique dessert and salad plates found at estate and garage
sales. Down the center of the table were candleholders from craft
stores, cake stands bearing cupcakes perched on upside-down teacups,
pastel-painted Mason jars holding flowers and a large white pitcher
filled with wildflowers as a centerpiece. Benches were used for seating,

covered with old quilts and decorative throw pillows. Around the room, vintage frames held photos of the happy couple.

This is the perfect opportunity to use the family dishes and linens stored away in the attic or closets, if you have them. If not, trawl antique stores and resale shops, which often have stashes of tablecloths, napkins and embroidered dishtowels. Look for real linen or finely woven cotton, lace, embroidery, hemstitching. Don't worry about a few small stains, and don't be afraid to repurpose: Linen handkerchiefs, once such an essential of every genteel wardrobe, make charming napkins; if you should find beautifully embroidered old pillowcases and sheets, they can make lovely placemats and tablecloths.

Plain white dinner plates can be combined with antique salad, dessert and appetizer plates, silverware and service pieces. Don't worry if things don't match or if they show some wear: That's part of the charm. For serving, use vintage platters, cake stands, footed bowls; offer the drinks in assorted goblets and stemmed glassware.

For table décor, play off the contrast of elegant and casual. Bunch more rustic flora like herbs, dried lavender and wildflowers in your fanciest vases. Alternatively, put roses, tulips and more elegant flowers in simple glass vases or old Mason jars. Mix short and tall in your floral arrangements, using vintage teapots, creamers, bud vases, urns and assorted crystal.

MIMOSA BAR

Impress your guests with a serve-yourself mimosa bar. Offer a variety of juices and fresh fruits for a twist on the traditional cocktail of orange juice and sparkling wine. Bonus: Alcohol-abstaining guests won't feel slighted, with all the juices available for sipping from festive flutes or coupes.

Generally a mimosa is half juice and half sparkling wine. If you're using standard 6-oz. flutes, 1 bottle of sparkling wine will make about 8 mimosas. Calculating 2 mimosas per person, a group of 20 people would need 5 bottles of sparkling wine. If you're offering 4 different flavors of juice, a quart of each should be adequate, but with all ingredients it's best to have extra, especially if guests are serving themselves, and one or two of the varieties will likely be more popular than the others.

Use a sparkling wine you wouldn't mind drinking by itself, but anything too elegant or pricey would be wasted in a mixed drink. An inexpensive Spanish cava is a good choice. Be sure the wine and the juices are thoroughly chilled (you can even put the juices in the freezer for 15 minutes or so before the party is to begin; set them out just before the guests arrive and refresh with chilled juice periodically).

Bottles of sparkling wine, chilled

Variety of fresh fruit juices, chilled (orange, pineapple, grapefruit, cranberry, pomegranate, mango, melon)

Variety of fresh fruit in bite-sized pieces (berries; mango wedges; pineapple chunks; sections of oranges, lemons and limes; melon chunks)

Arrange chilled bottles of sparkling wine in a large metal tub or ice buckets with ice and a little water. Pour chilled juice into decorative bottles or pitchers. Arrange bowls of fresh fruit in front of the juice lineup. Cluster flutes and/or coupes to the side; if you don't have these, white-wine glasses will do.

Hand-letter or print out a decorative sign to place on the mimosa bar that guides guests on what to do: "Pour some bubbly, splash some juice, garnish with fruit, bottoms up!" You can use a chalkboard for the sign and decorative labels for the juices and fruit if you like; you can also find printable signs and labels for a mimosa bar on the internet.

CLASSIC DEVILED EGGS

The tried-and-true original recipe, but dressed up with a piped filling.

Yield: 12 servings

6 hard-cooked eggs
1/3 cup mayonnaise
2 teaspoons yellow mustard
1/4 teaspoon paprika, plus more for garnish
1/4 teaspoon salt
1/4 teaspoon pepper

Cut the eggs in half and place the yolks in a bowl. Set the whites aside.

Add the mayonnaise, mustard, paprika, salt and pepper to the yolks. Mash together with a fork until mixture is smooth and combined completely.

Spoon the mixture into a piping bag fitted with a star tip and pipe the filling into the egg whites.

Arrange on a platter and garnish eggs with additional paprika and black pepper.

Variations to try:

Deviled eggs can be dressed up with all kinds of additions: Dijon or flavored mustards instead of yellow mustard; fresh herbs such as Italian parsley, basil, tarragon, chives or dill; aromatic spices such as curry powder or Spanish smoked paprika; finely chopped nuts; Asian flavors such as toasted sesame oil, soy sauce or wasabi; Mediterranean additions such as finely chopped black olives, sun-dried tomatoes and pine nuts; pickles or relishes such as capers or chutney – really, the possibilities are almost endless.

You can also change the flavor profile by adding yogurt, sour cream, cream cheese or soft goat cheese instead of (or in addition to) mayonnaise. Sherry vinegar or a little lemon juice can give the yolks a welcome edge of tartness. Here are a couple of variations, including an unusual maple-cinnamon one for those sweet of tooth, as many Texans are.

Smoked Salmon: Combine 6 egg yolks, 1/4 cup cream cheese, 1/2 teaspoon dry mustard and enough lemon juice to moisten yolks. Mash together until blended and smooth; garnish with fine-cut strips of smoked salmon. Finely chopped red onion, capers and fresh dill are classic additions to the yolks, too, and a tiny feather of dill makes a perfect garnish.

No-Yolk Deviled Eggs: Save the yolks for egg salad later and fill centers of eggs with something else entirely: guacamole garnished with a bit of pico de gallo; hummus topped with chives or with a cherry tomato half; herb-garnished potato salad.

Maple-Cinnamon: Combine 6 egg yolks, 1/4 cup cream cheese, 2 tablespoons maple syrup, 2 teaspoons honey mustard, 1/2 teaspoon cinnamon; mash until smooth. Garnish with finely chopped toasted pecans.

BLUEBERRY BLUE-CORN MUFFINS

Adding sugar to cornbread is almost blasphemous in Texas, but these corn muffins deserve a touch of honey for a special occasion. To serve, stack the muffins in a pyramid shape on a cake stand. If you can lay your hands on a mini muffin pan, make the minis instead of the larger muffins; they are handier to serve (and eat) at a gathering and look cuter to boot.

Yield: 12 large or 24 mini muffins

Cooking oil for pan

1 cup blue cornmeal (see note)

1/2 cup flour

1 tablespoon baking powder

1/2 teaspoon baking soda

1/2 teaspoon salt

1 cup buttermilk

1/2 cup whole milk

1 egg, lightly beaten

1/4 cup butter, melted

1 tablespoon honey

1/2 cup fresh blueberries, roughly chopped

Preheat oven to 425°; grease cups of muffin pan with cooking spray (or insert paper liners).

In a mixing bowl, combine the cornmeal, flour, baking powder, baking soda and salt.

In another bowl, blend remaining ingredients. Stir wet ingredients into dry ingredients until thoroughly blended; pour into cups of prepared muffin tin.

Bake for about 10 minutes, watching closely so that muffins don't over-brown.

NOTE: Blue cornmeal, ground from blue corn varieties originally cultivated by native Americans, can be found in the baking aisles of most larger supermarkets and health-food stores, or online.

BAKED MEXICAN FRITTATA WITH HASH-BROWN CRUST

A frittata is basically a quiche without a crust, but this recipe includes hash browns that sink to the bottom and become something even better than crust. Serve the frittata on a cake stand or round platter with salsa drizzled around the plate; cut frittata into wedges for serving.

Yield: 8 servings

1 1/2 cups frozen hash brown potatoes, undefrosted

2 tablespoons vegetable oil, plus more for greasing oven pan

1/2 cup crumbled Mexican chorizo (see note)

6 eggs

1 cup milk

1 teaspoon salt

1 teaspoon black pepper

1/2 cup prepared pico de gallo

1 cup grated sharp Cheddar cheese

1/2 cup grated Cotija cheese (see note)

2 whole jalapeños (red ones are particularly festive)

Salsa, for serving

Pat the frozen hash browns dry with a paper towel. In a large sauté pan over medium heat, add oil and brown the potatoes according to package directions. Remove potatoes and drain on paper toweling.

In the same pan, brown the chorizo, stirring frequently. Remove when browned and drain on paper toweling.

Preheat oven to 375°.

In a large bowl, thoroughly combine the eggs, milk, salt and pepper. Stir in the pico de gallo and cheeses.

Grease a 9-inch pie plate or tart pan. Spread the potatoes over the bottom of the pan, top with the drained crumbled chorizo and slowly pour the egg mixture over all. Bake for 10 minutes.

Meanwhile, cut the tops off the jalapenos; using a small knife, scrape out the seeds and discard (you can leave the seeds in if you know all your guests enjoy spicy-hot food, but it's safer to remove them). Slice jalapeños into thin rounds. Remove the frittata from the oven and gently lay the jalapeno rounds on the surface of the frittata, spacing evenly. Return frittata to oven and bake for an additional 15 to 20 minutes, or until just firm. Let cool slightly. Slice and serve with your favorite salsa.

NOTE: This recipe calls for Mexican chorizo, a fresh sausage that can be crumbled after you remove the casing — not Spanish chorizo, a denser cured and dried sausage. Cotija cheese is a hard, crumbly Mexican cow's milk cheese. Both are typically available in markets that count Hispanics among their clientele. If you can't find the Cotija, you can substitute crumbled feta or goat cheese.

WILDFLOWER HONEY GRANOLA PARFAIT

Build these parfaits in wine goblets, brandy glasses or stemmed dessert bowls. You can also use vintage coffee or tea cups, but clear vessels show off the layers. For drama, you could also build one large parfait in a trifle dish, but in that case you should double the recipe to create extra layers.

Yield: 4 to 6 individual parfaits

2 cups plain granola

2 tablespoons Texas wildflower honey, plus more for drizzling

2 cups frozen or fresh mixed berries

2 cups unflavored 2 percent yogurt

Edible flowers and mint leaves, for garnish

Preheat oven to 350°.

Place the granola in a mixing bowl; drizzle with honey and stir to combine. Spread granola onto a baking sheet lined with parchment paper and lightly toast in oven for 2 to 3 minutes. Remove from oven and cool completely.

Build the parfaits by layering berries, yogurt and granola until glass is full. Garnish with a drizzle of honey, mint leaves and an edible flower.

Note: Edible flowers can be purchased in the produce section of specialty food stores. If none can be found, save back a few of the berries and use them for garnish, along with the mint leaves.

STRAWBERRY CHESS SQUARES

Everyone loves lemon bars, but when I was growing up I wanted everything to be strawberry. This version is pretty, pink and delicious, perfect for a bridal brunch.

Yield: About 24 2-inch squares

CRUST
15.25-oz. box yellow cake mix

1 egg

1 stick (1/2 cup) butter, melted

TOPPING
3 eggs

8 oz. cream cheese, at room temperature

3 1/2 cups powdered sugar, plus more for garnish, if desired

1 tablespoon lemon juice

3 tablespoons strawberry jam

ASSEMBLY
Fresh strawberries, halved or thinly sliced vertically, for garnish, optional

Preheat oven to 350°.

CRUST

In a mixing bowl, combine the cake mix, egg and melted butter. Stir until completely combined. Press into a 9-by-13-inch pan.

TOPPING

In another bowl, use an electric mixer to beat the eggs; then beat in the cream cheese, powdered sugar, lemon juice and strawberry jam.

ASSEMBLY

Pour topping on top of the cake mixture and spread evenly with an offset spatula. Bake for 30 to 40 minutes. Let cool for at least 1 hour. Cut into squares before removing from the pan and sprinkle with additional powdered sugar, if desired. If you like, top each square with a strawberry half or with a fan of three thin strawberry slices.

CHAPTER 3
BOOTS & BLING BARBECUE

MENU

Blackberry Margaritas • Texas Summer Shandy • Big Bold BBQ Layered Dip • Grilled Butterflied Chicken • Bourbon-Braised Short Ribs Mom's Potato Salad • Sweet and Crunchy Coleslaw • Pecan Pie Shortbread Cookies

Most cowgirls like to break out the bling every now and then, and a Saturday night gathering for barbecue can the perfect occasion to show off one's flashiest Western wear.

Be sure to let your guests know that your dinner will be an occasion for their fanciest Western duds. This is no time for your working boots — pull out that special pair in exotic skins, bright colors and decorative stitching. Dress up your denim with statement turquoise jewelry, a satin rodeo shirt, jeweled belt buckle and a sparkly hatband on the cowboy hat.

There needs to be lots of sparkle on the table, too. Turquoise and metallics make for an unexpected color scheme — silver pairs particularly well with turquoise, as a glance at many a cowgirl's jewelry box will attest. Look for turquoise bandanas to use as napkins; tuck them under horseshoes spray-painted silver and glue-gunned with craft-store rhinestones, or buy toy spurs into which you can tuck the bandanas and fan them out. More simply, roll up each bandana and wrap and tie a leather cord spray-painted metallic and centered with turquoise, metallic or sparkly beads around the middle.

For your table centerpieces, dig out those old boots that are too worn to repair, clean them up and, if you think they need some enhancement, spray-paint them in a metallic shade or in a shade of turquoise that coordinates with the napkins. Place a cylindrical vase inside each boot and fill with bold flowers such as sunflowers or dahlias (keep the flowers in the same color family for maximum impact). You could accent the bouquets with graceful grass seedheads, also spray-painted metallic.

For candleholders, string jute twine with metallic, crystal and pearl beads, leaving spaces in between. Wrap the twine around a Mason jar and glue into place; place a flameless candle in each jar. Pick up a couple of stainless-steel feed buckets at the feed store and decorate them similarly for ice buckets.

Although the food is casual, the "bling" theme calls for service pieces as decorative as the rest of the table: crystal bowls for the sides, silver platters for the meat, cake stands for dessert. Set places with silver- or gold-colored chargers topped with Fiestaware-style pottery plates in colors coordinating with the rest of your table. Vintage enamelware camping plates would fit the theme too, if you're lucky enough to have a set. Cocktails can be made in festive glass pitchers and poured into goblets or margarita glasses and pilsner glasses – use inexpensive ones and bling them up with rhinestone-and-glue-gun or jute-and-beads embellishment.

As for the menu, here's a meaty triple play starring not one but three barbecue favorites — pork, chicken and beef ribs, plus the two classic side dishes no barbecue can be without. A rich baked layered dip that rings all the comfort-food bells kicks things off, and dessert's a riff on Texas' most famous sweet — pecan pie — so tell your guests to bring their best appetites (you could, of course, dial back to a one-entrée menu). Meanwhile, the cocktails tick off both barbecue beverage boxes with beer and margaritas; have plenty of iced tea on hand, too.

The bonus with all these recipes is that they can be made in advance: The cookies can be baked up to a month ahead and frozen. The chicken and ribs can be kept warm in the oven; the dip starts in a slow cooker and can be assembled the day before; and the salads taste better after refrigerating for a few hours — which leaves a cowgirl plenty of time for primping.

BLACKBERRY MARGARITAS

Yield: 6 cocktails

3 limes
3/4 cup blackberries
3 tablespoons sugar
1 cup ice, plus more for glasses
2/3 cup tequila
1/3 cup orange liqueur
1/3 cup amaretto

Juice 2 limes into a quart-size pitcher and slice the last lime into 6 wedges for garnish. Reserve 6 unblemished berries for garnish.

Add the rest of the blackberries and the sugar to the pitcher. Using a muddler, mash the blackberries. Add ice, tequila, orange liqueur and amaretto. Stir vigorously for 15 to 20 seconds to chill the cocktail.

Fill 4 glasses with ice and strain liquid into the glasses. Garnish each glass with a blackberry and a lime wedge.

TEXAS SUMMER SHANDY

Yield: 6 cocktails

24 oz. lager-style beer
1 cup apple or orange juice
1 cup lemonade
1 cup ginger ale
6 lemon wedges, for garnish

In a pitcher, combine the beer, juice and lemonade. Stir to combine; then add the ginger ale. Pour into ice-filled highball glasses; garnish glasses with lemon wedges.

BIG BOLD BBQ LAYERED DIP

Pulled pork, the Texas way, really should be cooked low and slow in a smoker for several hours. But a slow cooker provides an easy alternative if you do not have access to a smoker. I created this hot and hearty crunchy-creamy-cheesy dip to showcase the sauce from Stanley's Famous Pit Barbecue in Tyler, Texas. Serving East Texas for more than 50 years, owners Nick and Jen Pencis have won the praise of barbecue aficionados throughout the state and nationwide. The Stanley's sauce is thinner than most and boasts rich flavors of tomato, molasses, paprika, pepper and other spices. It leans heavy on the vinegar and even has a touch of anchovy puree. I prefer their sauce above all others, but if it's not available in your area, use your personal favorite — choose one that's on the tart rather than the sweet side, though.

Yield: 12 cups

2-pound pork tenderloin roast

1 teaspoon salt

1 teaspoon pepper

1 teaspoon garlic powder

1 cup water

1 cup barbecue sauce

1 yellow onion

1 egg

1/2 cup milk

1 cup flour

Oil for frying

2 cups cooked mashed potatoes

8 ounces sour cream

2 cups grated Cheddar cheese

Rub the pork with salt, pepper and garlic powder and place in a slow cooker. Add water and cook on low for 4 to 6 hours, until meat is tender and can be shredded with two forks. Finely shred all the meat and stir in the barbecue sauce. Remove from slow cooker and let cool to room temperature.

Meanwhile, slice the onion thinly. In a bowl large enough to hold all the onion slices, stir together the egg and milk. Spread the flour onto a dinner plate. Line another plate with paper towels to drain the fried onion rings. In a deep skillet, heat 1/2 inch of oil over high heat to 325°. Thoroughly coat the onion slices in the egg-milk mixture. Pick up a handful of onion slices, shake off the excess liquid, dredge in the flour and add to the oil. Cook until golden and crisp; remove the fried onions and drain on paper towels. Repeat until all onions are coated and fried.

In a 9-by-13-inch baking dish attractive enough for serving, spread the mashed potatoes on the bottom, cover with the pork and sauce, then the sour cream and then the cheese. Top with the fried onions. Cover dish with foil and refrigerate until an hour before guests arrive.

An hour before serving, remove dip from fridge and let sit, covered with foil, 30 minutes to come to room temperature. Meanwhile, preheat oven to 350°. Bake dip covered for 20 minutes; then remove foil and return dish to oven for the last 10 minutes. Serve with sturdy chips for dipping; for testing purposes, Frito Scoops were used. Be sure to warn guests not to touch the hot baking dish at first.

GRILLED BUTTERFLIED CHICKEN

This is one of my favorite ways to cook a whole chicken. Cooking it flat takes less time than roasting a whole chicken in the oven. This method also leaves the chicken juicy and full of flavor from the grill.

Yield: 4 to 6 servings
1 lemon, halved
1/4 cup olive oil
1 tablespoon brown sugar
1 teaspoon coarse salt
1 teaspoon cracked black pepper
1 teaspoon smoked paprika
1 teaspoon dried parsley
1/2 teaspoon garlic powder
1 whole chicken (5 to 6 pounds)

Juice half the lemon into a small bowl, reserving the other half. Whisk the olive oil, brown sugar, salt, pepper, paprika, parsley and garlic powder into the lemon juice.

Place the chicken on a baking sheet, back side up. Use kitchen shears or a sharp knife to cut out the backbone of the chicken: Starting at the tail, cut right next to the backbone up one side of the backbone; repeat on the other side. Discard the backbone.

Spread the chicken flat, skin side down, and rub all over with the oil and seasoning mixture. Turn breast side up and rub the mixture over the top and underneath the skin.

Clean the surface of the grill and heat grill to high. Set grill up for indirect-heat cooking by repositioning coals to the sides of the grill, leaving a space in the middle over which the chicken will be cooked, or by turning down the heat on one side of the grill to low. Place the chicken, skin side down, on the low-heat part of the grill. Close the lid and grill until the skin is nicely charred and crispy, about 15 minutes; watch for flare-ups and spray with a water bottle, if necessary.

Carefully flip the chicken and continue to cook with the grill lid closed until the chicken is cooked through, an additional 20 to 30 minutes, depending on size of chicken. When an instant-read thermometer inserted into the thickest part of the thigh reaches 165°, remove chicken from the grill and let rest uncovered for 10 minutes before slicing. Just before serving, squeeze remaining lemon half over sliced chicken.

BOURBON-BRAISED SHORT RIBS

Yield: 4 servings

2 tablespoons steak seasoning blend

1 tablespoon garlic powder

1 tablespoon dry mustard

2 teaspoons coarse sea salt

8 beef short ribs

1 cup flour

1/4 cup vegetable oil

1 large onion, sliced thin

4 cloves garlic, minced

1/2 cup bourbon

3 cups beef broth, warmed

2 chipotles in adobo sauce, roughly chopped

2 tablespoons brown sugar

2 teaspoons butter, optional

Preheat oven to 350°. In a small bowl, combine the steak seasoning, garlic powder, dry mustard and salt. Rub the ribs with this seasoning mixture on both sides.

Place flour in a shallow bowl. In a large deep skillet, heat the oil over high heat until it sizzles when a pinch of flour is sprinkled in. Dredge each short rib in the flour, shaking off the excess before placing the rib in the oil. Sear the ribs until they are browned on all sides; then transfer to a 9-by-13-inch baking dish.

When all ribs are seared, reduce heat to medium and add the onion slices to the pan. Sauté until softened; then add the garlic and sauté for an additional minute. Remove the skillet from the heat and let cool for 1 minute. (This will keep the bourbon from flaming.) Add the bourbon, swirl and scrape the bottom of the pan. Place skillet back on the heat. Add the broth, chipotles and brown sugar and stir until brown sugar is dissolved.

Pour the hot liquid over the ribs. Cover the dish with foil and bake in 350° oven for 2 hours, or until the meat is tender and about to fall off the bone. Transfer the ribs to a serving dish and cover with foil.

Strain the sauce into a saucepan and place the saucepan over high heat. Bring the sauce to a boil and reduce to half its volume. Taste the sauce and adjust seasoning with salt and pepper. If flavor seems harsh, stir in 2 teaspoons of butter to soften the flavor. Pour sauce over the ribs and serve.

MOM'S POTATO SALAD

I have never found another potato salad that is as good as my mother's. Nothing comes close to comparing, and now that she has shared her recipe with me I have figured out why. The secret to this recipe is sprinkling the potatoes with vinegar and sugar immediately after cooking and draining. Then you place them in the freezer to cool them down quickly. This keeps the potatoes from turning to mush when you stir in the other ingredients and infuses great flavor into the potatoes.

Yield: 6 to 8 servings

8 medium red potatoes
1 tablespoon sugar

1 tablespoon white vinegar

1/2 teaspoon salt

2 hard-boiled eggs, chopped

1/4 cup finely chopped sweet pickles

1/4 cup finely chopped celery

1/2 cup mayonnaise

1 tablespoon mustard

1/2 teaspoon paprika

1/2 teaspoon black pepper

Peel potatoes and cut into 1/2-inch chunks. Place potatoes in a large pot and add cold water to cover by 2 inches. Bring to a boil, lower heat to a brisk simmer, cover and cook until potatoes are fork-tender, about 15 to 20 minutes.

Drain the potatoes well and transfer to a large bowl. Immediately sprinkle with sugar, vinegar and salt and gently toss to distribute. Place in the freezer for 30 minutes.

After the potatoes have chilled, add the chopped hard-boiled eggs, sweet pickles and celery. Gently stir in the mayonnaise, mustard, paprika and pepper. Taste for seasoning and add additional salt, pepper or paprika if needed. Chill for at least 2 hours or overnight.

SWEET AND CRUNCHY COLESLAW

*Here's a lighter version of traditional coleslaw that offers a little
sweetness and extra crunch.*

Yield: 8 to 10 servings

DRESSING

1/4 cup apple-cider vinegar

1/4 cup grapeseed or vegetable oil

2 tablespoons mayonnaise

1 tablespoon Dijon mustard

1 tablespoon honey

1/2 teaspoon salt

1/4 teaspoon black pepper

SLAW

1/2 head napa cabbage, cored, any damaged outer leaves discarded

1/2 head red cabbage, cored, any damaged outer leaves discarded

2 carrots, peeled

2 apples, cored (peeled or unpeeled, as you like)

1/3 cup dried cranberries, finely chopped

1/2 cup slivered almonds

DRESSING
Combine all ingredients in a jar with a secure screw top and shake
vigorously to mix thoroughly and emulsify.

SLAW

In a food processor fitted with the shredding attachment, shred the cabbages, carrots and apples.

Transfer shredded mixture to a large bowl. Pour enough of the dressing over the slaw to moisten the slaw completely, but not so much that the dressing pools in the bottom of the bowl (start with a small amount of dressing, toss to coat thoroughly as you go and add more dressing gradually). Add the cranberries and almonds and lightly toss to combine.

PECAN PIE SHORTBREAD COOKIES

When I need a recipe that is truly Texan, I go to the Go Texan website. Created by the Texas Department of Agriculture, it offers a database of recipes created by Texas chefs with ingredients grown in Texas. This is one of my favorites because it satisfies a pecan pie craving during any time of year, not just Thanksgiving.

COOKIES

1 cup packed brown sugar

3/4 cup butter, at room temperature

1 egg

1 teaspoon vanilla extract

2 cups flour

1 teaspoon baking powder

FILLING

1 cup chopped pecans

1/2 cup packed brown sugar

1/4 cup heavy cream

1 teaspoon vanilla extract

Preheat oven to 350°. Line 2 baking trays with parchment paper and set aside.

COOKIES

In a large mixing bowl, use an electric mixer to beat together the brown sugar, butter, egg and vanilla until creamy. Beat in the flour and baking powder until well mixed.

Shape the dough into 1-1/4-inch balls and place balls 2 inches apart onto baking trays. Make an indentation in each cookie with your thumb, rotating your thumb to hollow the indentation out slightly.

FILLING

In a small bowl, mix together all ingredients.

ASSEMBLY

Fill each cookie with 1 rounded teaspoon of filling. Bake for 8 to 12 minutes or until lightly browned. Cool for 1 minute before removing from cookie sheets with a spatula.

CHAPTER 4

SUNDAY CHURCH POTLUCK: CLASSIC CASSEROLES AND COVERED DISHES

MENU

Sweet Mint Iced Tea • Three-Bean Salad • Cheesy Pineapple Casserole • Asparagus Cheese Casserole • King Ranch Chicken • Slow Cooker Sunday Ham • Sweet-Potato Bread • Banana Bread Trifle • Dark-Chocolate Sheet Cake

We all know that Texas is God's country, where every good cowgirl spends Sunday morning and sometimes Wednesday evening singing praises to the Lord and mingling with fellow friends of faith. And, in my neck of the woods, faith, fellowship and food go hand in hand.

Whether it's a potluck dinner at the church, a Bible study gathering at someone's home or Sunday dinner with family and friends, the classic fare is casseroles and covered dishes.

Each of these recipes has been passed to me by one of my favorite church ladies, and I use that term in the most endearing way. These amazing ladies have been a loving influence in so many lives – not to mention the gooey, cheesy love that oozes from every casserole they prepare. Some may argue that these recipes need some updating, but they are dishes that have comforted a multitude of souls, and I feel presumptuous thinking I can improve on a recipe that has been shared countless times in the Sunday school room, over many generations.

These recipes for family classics were often rewritten on cute recipe cards and bequeathed to daughters and daughters-in-law as cooking primers. I remember carefully following the instructions on my mother's recipe card for King Ranch Chicken for my first dinner party in college, and basking in glowing reviews. If I'd been handed the recipe for a modern version with 23 ingredients, I'd probably have been so overwhelmed I'd've given up and ordered a pizza.

So, for the most part, I have stuck to the originals, because they represent comfort food at its best. Each bite conjures images of church dresses, buckled shoes, Grandma in pearls with matching purse and pumps, potlucks in the fellowship hall or the family around the dining-room table for Sunday dinner, with fried chicken on the good china.

I get excited every time I spy vintage Pyrex and bakeware in a thrift shop or antique store — I'm a sucker for any pattern that reminds me of my childhood or that one of my grandmothers would have admired. But choosing the proper potluck vessel usually involves a few questions: Does the dish need to stay warm? Are you guaranteed to get it back? Where are you taking it?

Keeping things warm is important because you might not have a chance to reheat once you reach your destination. That's why I love casserole dishes with lids. I have a couple of insulated carriers that fit a 9-by-13-inch pan, and they do a great job of holding heat for a few hours.

A big concern of any potluck event is retrieving your dish after it's been scraped clean. If it is a large event, then I would probably cook in and serve out of a disposable aluminum pan, but for more intimate gatherings, where you can keep track of your dish, you can never go wrong with traditional Pyrex.

Which brings me to where you are taking the dish and who is in attendance. For a "Sunday best" family supper, you can transport the food in plastic containers and bring a nice dish with you for serving. This works well for creamy salads and other non-casserole dishes. For casseroles, there are plenty of beautiful oven-to-table pieces that will suit any occasion.

You might even want to break out some of the "Sunday best" china if you want to impress the other ladies with more than just your cooking. If you do, though, I have one word of advice: Don't set your wedding-gift crystal trifle dish on the hood of the car while you're getting the kiddos loaded. I learned that lesson the hard way. Trifles are allowed to look a little messy, but "smashed on the driveway" gives a whole new meaning to the word.

SWEET MINT ICED TEA

All Texans fall into two categories: sweet and unsweetened — when it comes to iced tea, of course. I prefer unsweetened and was raised by parents who liked their tea so strong it could walk across the counter. But I know most Texans prefer sweet tea, so I compromise by making sweet tea but leaning to the conservative side on the sugar. The die-hard sweet-tea drinkers can always add more. Or you could make extra mint-sugar syrup and pass it in a little crystal pitcher at the table.

Yield: 10 cups

10 cups water, divided
1 cup sugar
15 fresh mint leaves
5 tea bags

Optional mint sprigs for garnish

Sliced lemons and additional sweetener, for serving

In a saucepan, combine add 2 cups of the water and the sugar. Bring to a boil and stir until mixture is clear. Remove from heat and add the mint leaves, pushing the leaves down into the syrup. Set aside to steep for 10 minutes.

In a large nonreactive saucepan, bring the remaining 8 cups water to a boil. Add the tea bags and remove from heat. Let steep for 5 minutes. Remove and discard bags and let the tea cool.

Pour cooled tea into a pitcher. Strain the mint leaves from the syrup; discard mint leaves and add the syrup to the tea, stirring to mix thoroughly. Chill completely and serve over ice, garnished with mint sprigs if desired. Pass lemons and sweetener at the table.

THREE-BEAN SALAD

If you ask my dad, this is my mother's most popular recipe. But I must confess — since we might be eating this in church — that it was never my favorite. Back then my palate could not appreciate the vinegar, but now I love it — after digging out this recipe card, I'll be making it at my next cookout.

Yield: 8 to 10 servings

15.5-oz. can cut green beans

15.5-oz. can cut yellow (or wax) beans

15.5-oz. can kidney beans

1 small onion, peeled and sliced thinly

1 small green bell pepper, cored and sliced

3/4 cup sugar

2/3 cup white-wine vinegar

1/3 cup canola oil

1 teaspoon salt

1/2 teaspoon black pepper

Drain all beans well. Place in large bowl and add sliced onion and bell pepper.

In a separate bowl, make dressing by whisking together remaining ingredients. Pour over beans and toss to coat. Cover and refrigerate for several hours or overnight.

KING RANCH CHICKEN

Growing up in Texas, I ate my mother's cheesy chicken casserole with tortillas all the time. It wasn't until college, where it appeared on the sorority house menu, that I realized this dish was not her creation. It had a name, and it was King Ranch Chicken – one of the most beloved casseroles of Texas. Indeed, this might be the quintessential Texas cowgirl recipe, even though its connections with the legendary King Ranch are tenuous. I can thank many Methodist church ladies for sharing this recipe with my sweet, beautiful, not-from-Texas mother.

Yield: 12 servings (unless you have brothers)

1/4 cup canola oil

10 flour tortillas

3 cups cooked chicken, chopped

10.75-oz. can cream of mushroom soup

10.75-oz. can cream of chicken soup

10-oz. can Ro*Tel Original tomatoes and green chiles

1 medium onion, peeled and thinly sliced

2 cups grated Cheddar cheese, divided

In a skillet, heat the oil over high heat. Begin adding the tortillas one at a time and let them crisp very briefly on each side, removing to paper towels to drain.

In a large bowl, combine the chicken, the soups, the Ro*Tel, the sliced onion and 1 cup of the grated Cheddar.

Preheat oven to 350°. Grease a 9-by-13-inch baking dish. Spread a layer of the chicken mixture on the bottom of the pan. Break the tortillas into large pieces and scatter half over the top of the chicken. Repeat layers with remaining chicken and remaining tortillas. Sprinkle with remaining 1 cup grated cheese on top. Bake for 30 minutes, or until top is golden and bubbly.

CHEESY PINEAPPLE CASSEROLE

Leave it to a casserole to combine unexpected flavors, and this one is the perfect example. Who knew pineapple and Cheddar could be so good together? This recipe comes from a woman who is like my third grandmother. Everything you associate with a grandmother – tea and cookies, azalea bushes in the front yard, sewing room filled with projects, lavender soap in the bathroom and a recipe box filled with the best comfort food in the world – she epitomizes. Here's to Mary Lynn Thompson, the most noble of women in God's eyes, the ultimate prayer warrior and the elite leader of the best Baptist Salad Supper group in all of Texas!

Yield: 9 servings

20-oz. can pineapple tidbits, drained
1 cup grated Cheddar cheese
1/2 cup sugar
3 tablespoons flour
1/2 cup (1 stick) butter, melted
1 sleeve Ritz or similar butter crackers, crushed

Preheat oven to 350°. Grease an 8-by-8-inch baking dish.

In a mixing bowl, mix pineapple and cheese together.

In a separate small bowl, combine the sugar and flour.

Stir sugar-flour mixture into the pineapple-cheese mixture, blend and pour into greased dish. Pour melted butter over the top and scatter with crushed crackers. Bake for 30 minutes.

ASPARAGUS CHEESE CASSEROLE

This was a favorite recipe from my Grammy that adorned the checkered-cloth tables of many Sunday potlucks and countless family dinners. Fresh asparagus is the primary choice in modern times, so — sorry, Grammy — I have updated the recipe to include fresh instead of canned. This casserole will make you say a prayer of thanksgiving for asparagus.

Yield: 9 servings

1 pound fresh asparagus spears

3 eggs, well beaten

1/2 teaspoon salt

1/4 teaspoon black pepper

1 cup milk

1 cup Swiss cheese, grated

1 cup freshly crushed Saltine crackers (about 20 crackers), divided

2 tablespoons melted butter

Set a pot of water on to boil over high heat and fill a bowl with ice water.

Trim the bottom inch or so from each asparagus spear and discard. Cut asparagus into 1-inch lengths.

When water is at a full boil, add the asparagus and cook only for 30 seconds; use a slotted spoon or sieve to remove the asparagus to the ice water. Allow to cool completely before draining well.

Meanwhile, preheat oven to 350° and grease an 8-by-8-inch baking dish.

In a large mixing bowl, thoroughly beat the eggs with the salt and pepper. Add milk, cheese, drained asparagus and 3/4 cup of the cracker crumbs. Stir to combine.

Pour into prepared baking dish. Scatter the remaining cracker crumbs over the top and drizzle with the butter. Bake for 50 to 60 minutes, until filling is set.

SLOW COOKER SUNDAY HAM

You can't have a potluck dinner without a slow cooker recipe, and this one is perfect. You'll need to prep the ham the night before, but then it can go into the slow cooker early in the morning and be ready by the time you get home from church. This recipe calls for a picnic ham, which is not technically a ham, as it is taken from the pig's front leg and shoulder rather than the back leg. But it is smoked like a ham, and this is the name it typically goes by in the United States. For testing purposes, I used a Smithfield Ready-to-Cook Smoked Pork Shoulder Picnic Ham split in half before packaging.

Yield: 1/2 pound serving per person

4- to 6-pound pork shoulder picnic ham

1/2 cup dark-brown sugar

1 tablespoon honey

1 tablespoon dry mustard

1/2 teaspoon black pepper

1/2 teaspoon chili powder

1/2 teaspoon ground cinnamon

1/2 cup balsamic vinegar

1/2 cup water

Trim some of the excess fat from the ham, leaving a layer about 1/4-inch thick. Using a small carving knife, score the skin of the ham in a crosshatch or diamond pattern all over. The pattern should have 1-inch-wide intervals and be about 1/3-inch deep. Place the ham, meat side down, in a 9-by-13-inch pan.

In a small bowl, combine the brown sugar, honey, dry mustard, black pepper, chili powder and cinnamon. Stir to combine and rub the mixture over the outside of the ham. Cover ham and refrigerate overnight.

You'll need about an hour per pound of ham in the slow cooker, so allow 4 to 6 hours for cooking, depending on the size of your ham. Place the ham in the slow cooker meat side down. Scrape any drippings or seasoning from the bottom of the pan into the slow cooker. Add the vinegar and water. Turn the slow cooker to low and cook for 4 to 6 hours, until meat is tender and juicy.

Remove ham from the slow cooker and place on a serving platter; tent with foil to keep warm.

Spoon the drippings and liquid out of the slow cooker into a large measuring cup. Place in the freezer for 10 minutes to allow the fat to separate. Spoon off the fat and discard. Pour the remaining liquid into a saucepan, bring to a boil and continue to boil until reduced and thickened to your desired sauce consistency. Taste sauce for seasoning. Remove foil from ham, baste the ham with some of the sauce and pass the remaining sauce at the table.

SWEET-POTATO BREAD

For optimum slicing, make this the day before you need it.

Yield: 1 loaf

3 medium sweet potatoes
2 cups flour, divided
1 cup dark-brown sugar
1 tablespoon baking powder

1/2 teaspoon ground cinnamon

1/2 teaspoon salt

1/4 teaspoon baking soda

1/2 cup milk

2 eggs

1/3 cup Crisco

1/2 cup chopped pecans

Peel the sweet potatoes and cut into large chunks. Place in a saucepan and cover with water. Cover pan and bring to a boil, then lower heat to a simmer and cook about 20 minutes, until the potatoes are fork-tender. Drain sweet potatoes and mash with a potato masher to a smooth consistency. Measure out 2 cups of mashed sweet potatoes and set aside (save any excess for another use, or discard).

Preheat oven to 350° and grease a 9-by-5-by-3-inch loaf pan.

In a large mixing bowl, combine 1 cup of the flour with the brown sugar, baking powder, cinnamon, salt and baking soda. Stir in the mashed sweet potatoes, milk, eggs and Crisco.

Beat with an electric mixer on low speed until blended. Add the remaining 1 cup flour, turn the mixer to high and beat for 2 minutes. Stir in the pecans.

Pour batter into greased pan and bake for 60 minutes, or until a toothpick inserted into the middle comes out clean. Cool for 10 minutes, then remove loaf from the pan. Allow loaf to cool completely, wrap in plastic and store overnight before slicing.

BANANA BREAD TRIFLE

Banana pudding is a longstanding staple in the South, and everyone loves banana bread. This recipe brings the two together. This trifle is also beautiful when layered in wine goblets, clear dessert dishes or sherbet glasses for individual desserts.

Yield: 8 to 10 servings

3-oz. box banana-flavored pudding and pie filling

3 cups whipped cream, divided

4 bananas, sliced, divided

1 loaf banana bread, cut into 1-inch cubes, divided

20 vanilla wafers, crushed

Prepare the banana pudding according to package directions. Fold in 1 cup of the whipped cream and 3 of the sliced bananas.

Cover the bottom of a trifle dish or large glass bowl with a layer of banana-bread cubes. Top with 1 cup of banana pudding mixture. Continue to layer until all banana bread and pudding is used. Top with remaining 2 cups whipped cream, garnish with remaining banana slices and sprinkle with the crushed vanilla wafers. Refrigerate until ready to serve.

DARK-CHOCOLATE SHEET CAKE

Every time we went to my grandmother's house my mother had to make this cake. Chocolate sheet cake (sometimes quaintly called "sheath cake") is a Texas classic, and this one is super-rich. Chocoholics will not be disappointed.

Yield: 20 servings

CAKE

1/2 cup Crisco

1/2 cup (1 stick) butter

4 tablespoons cocoa powder

1 cup water

2 cups sugar

2 cups flour

1 teaspoon baking soda

1/2 cup buttermilk

2 eggs

1 teaspoon vanilla

FROSTING

1/2 cup (1 stick) butter

4 tablespoons cocoa powder

4 tablespoons milk

3 1/2 cups powdered sugar

1 cup chopped pecans

CAKE

Preheat oven to 400°. Grease and flour a 9-by-13-inch baking pan.

In a saucepan, combine Crisco, butter, cocoa and water. Bring to a boil, stir to blend completely and set aside.

In large mixing bowl, combine sugar, flour and baking soda. Using an electric mixer, blend in buttermilk and eggs, then vanilla. Mix until all ingredients are incorporated and consistency is creamy. Add the boiled shortening-and-cocoa mixture and blend thoroughly.

Pour batter into greased pan and bake for 25 minutes, or until a toothpick inserted in the middle of the cake comes out clean. Allow to cool completely in the pan before frosting.

FROSTING

Combine butter, cocoa and milk in a saucepan. Bring to a boil. Immediately remove from heat and stir in powdered sugar, mixing well; then stir in pecans. Spread over top of cake in pan.

CHAPTER 5
FOURTH OF JULY FISH FRY

MENU

Strawberry Lemonade • Watermelon-Lime Rickey • Corn and Crab-Claw Fritters • Grilled Green-Tomato Caprese Salad • Tex-Mex Fish & Chips • Cornmeal-Crusted Okra Fries • Grilled Corn With Chile-Lime Butter • Red, White and Blue Pie

There are lots of advantages to being a Texas cowgirl who enjoys life in the country. Wide-open spaces and plenty of four-legged friends come to mind, but another plus is being outside the city limits on the Fourth of July. It's a Texas tradition that if you live in the country you put on your own fireworks show.

Dad would go to the fireworks stand and buy all his favorites — enough for an hour of noisy, smoky fun. It was one the best days of summer – all those red, white and blue decorations; plenty of fun food to eat; and, for some lucky cowgirls, a trip to the lake or the beach, with fireworks to come.

Some of my favorite summers were spent near the Gulf Coast, where we would fill our days with crabbing and fishing expeditions. I was one of the few 8-year-old kids who would turn down a hot dog in favor of boiled crab and fried okra. That's why a fish fry on the Fourth of July seems just as traditional to me as hot dogs, hamburgers and potato salad.

For this Texas Gulf Coast menu, I'd suggest investing in an outdoor fryer from a local sporting-goods store. It's easier to clean up than an indoor fryer, and the capacity is much larger. Just be sure to follow instructions and pay close attention to all of the safety precautions.

In the kitchen, you might consider also using a large, deep skillet or Dutch oven to fry the okra and the fritters. Once you start frying, you can't walk away, so designate two people to "man the fryers" and coordinate the breading process. The fritters can be made first and served early for guests to nibble on while the fish and chips and the okra are being prepared. To keep things warm, heat your oven to 200° and line baking sheets with parchment paper so you can hold items in the oven until you are ready to serve.

For the party décor, go all out with flags, bunting, streamers and anything you have that's red, white or blue — the Fourth is not the occasion for understated elegance. Visit a craft or party store for patriotic drink umbrellas, straws, napkins, plates, table covers, pinwheels, paper lanterns and plenty of flags.

For serving, look for plastic burger and hot-dog baskets — red is traditional, but they're available in blue as well — along with paper liners in coordinating checks. To decorate the tables, fill glass containers with red, white and blue hard candies and vases with white daisies, mums or hydrangeas (tuck in a few sparklers, if you like, to light after the meal, when it's getting dark). Mix in a few Texas flags with the Stars and Stripes, and you've got yourself a Texas-style Independence Day celebration.

STRAWBERRY LEMONADE

Yield: About 14 cups

12 cups water, divided

1 1/2 cups sugar

2 cups hulled and sliced strawberries

1 1/2 cups fresh lemon juice

Lemon wedges and/or whole strawberries for garnish

Make simple syrup: In a medium saucepan, combine 2 cups water and the sugar. Bring to a simmer and stir until the mixture is clear. Set aside to cool.

Place the strawberries and lemon juice in a blender and puree until smooth. Strain if desired. Pour into a large pitcher and stir in the simple syrup. Add remaining 10 cups water, stir to blend, and chill.

When ready to serve, stir lemonade well. Add ice to glasses and pour in lemonade. Garnish each with a lemon wedge and/or a whole strawberry.

WATERMELON-LIME RICKEY

A rickey is a refreshing cocktail that typically contains gin, lime and club soda. Of course, it's not July Fourth until someone cuts open a cold watermelon, so when you add watermelon to the formula, it's the perfect way to celebrate and beat the Texas heat.

Yield: About 6 cups

3 cups ice

2 cups club soda

2 cups cubed watermelon (from about a 1 1/2-pound watermelon)

1/2 cup gin

1/3 cup sugar

1/4 cup fresh lime juice

Lime wedges for garnish

Combine all ingredients in a blender and blend until smooth. Serve garnished with lime wedges.

CORN AND CRAB-CLAW FRITTERS

This recipe started as my Grammy's corn fritters, but after a few years of Gulf Coast living I decided crabmeat would be a great addition. You can adjust the amount of crab to your taste. If you are serving the fritters as appetizers, make them on the small side, as finger food; for a side dish, make them larger.

Yield: About 12 fritters, 1 1/2 to 2 inches each

2 eggs

2 cups fresh corn kernels or frozen or canned whole-kernel corn

1/2 cup claw crabmeat

1/2 teaspoon salt

1/2 teaspoon pepper

1 1/4 cups flour

1 teaspoon baking powder

Vegetable oil, for frying

In a large bowl, beat eggs well; blend in corn, crabmeat, salt and pepper.

In a separate bowl or onto a sheet of waxed paper, sift together flour and baking powder. Stir into corn mixture until thoroughly blended.

In a deep skillet, heat 2 inches of cooking oil over high heat. When a bit of the batter dropped into the oil sizzles immediately, the oil is hot enough. Working in batches (do not crowd the skillet), drop tablespoons of batter into the oil and cook for 2 to 3 minutes or until golden. Remove to a plate lined with paper towels.

GRILLED GREEN-TOMATO CAPRESE SALAD

In Texas we like our fried food, but we also like our fresh summer vegetables. Using tart green tomatoes sweetened and softened on the grill adds an unexpected twist.

Yield: 10 to 12 servings

5 small to medium green tomatoes

1/4 cup extra-virgin olive oil, plus extra for drizzling

2 (1/2-pound) balls of fresh mozzarella

About 2 dozen fresh basil leaves, plus some sprigs for garnish

Salt and pepper, to taste

Balsamic vinegar, for drizzling

Grated parmesan, for garnish

Heat a grill or grill pan to high. Slice off and discard the top of each tomato, as well as a small slice from the bottom, so that you can cut even slices. Cut the tomatoes into 1/2-inch slices; you should have about 2 dozen, depending on the size of the tomatoes. Brush the tomato slices with the olive oil on both sides. When grill is very hot, add the tomato slices. Grill for 20 seconds each side.

Slice the mozzarella balls thinly; you want roughly the same number of mozzarella slices as tomato slices.

Begin building the salad on the plate you will be using to serve; a large round plate or a long platter works best. For round, make an overlapping circle in the center of the plate, starting with a grilled tomato slice, then a slice of mozzarella and then a basil leaf. Repeat with as many circles as needed, radiating outward, to use all tomatoes, cheese and basil. For a long platter, make two or three long overlapping rows.

Sprinkle with salt and freshly ground pepper and garnish with a generous drizzle of olive oil, drops of balsamic vinegar, a sprinkling of freshly grated parmesan and some extra basil leaves.

TEX-MEX FISH & CHIPS

The simple addition of taco seasoning turns everyday fish and chips into the best fish and chips your guests have ever tasted. This is also my secret batter for fish tacos: Just slice the fish into smaller strips.

Yield: 8 servings

Vegetable oil, for frying

2 pounds fresh cod

2 cups flour

1.25-oz. packet taco seasoning, divided

1 1/2 cups light beer

6 red potatoes

1/2 teaspoon salt

1/2 teaspoon black pepper

Preheat oven to 200° and line a baking sheet with paper towels. Heat oil in a deep fryer (or 2 inches of oil in a deep skillet) over high heat. Oil will be ready for frying at around 350°; use a candy thermometer to gauge the temperature.

Slice the fish into 2-inch strips.

In a medium bowl, mix the flour with 1 tablespoon of the taco seasoning. Add the beer and whisk until there are no clumps. Immediately begin dipping the fish in the batter and placing it in the hot oil. Fry in batches if necessary to maintain the 350° temperature; do not crowd the fryer or skillet. Fry the fish for about 3 minutes, removing to paper-towel-lined baking sheet when golden. Place baking sheet in 200-degree oven to keep warm.

To make the chips, sieve out any bits of fish or batter from the oil and reheat to 350°. Quarter potatoes lengthwise, slide the wedges into the oil (do not crowd) and fry for about 2 minutes, removing to a paper-towel-lined plate when golden-brown. While potatoes are frying, in a small bowl, combine the remaining taco seasoning, salt and pepper; sprinkle this mixture over the potatoes as soon as they come out of the oil.

CORNMEAL-CRUSTED OKRA FRIES

This is not your typical fried okra, but I like it because the crust is light and crispy and because splitting the okra lengthwise means you can serve them like French fries. Make sure you use young, small pods.

Yield: 48 okra fries

2 dozen small okra pods

2 cups yellow cornmeal

1/2 cup flour

1 teaspoon salt

1 teaspoon black pepper

6 egg whites

1/3 cup water

Vegetable oil, for frying

Cut okra pods in half lengthwise.

In a large bowl, stir together the cornmeal, flour, salt and pepper to combine. In another bowl, stir together the egg whites and water.

Heat oil in a deep fryer (or 2 inches of oil in a deep skillet) over high heat. Oil temperature should be around 350° to fry; use a candy thermometer to gauge the temperature.

Dip each piece of okra into the egg-white mixture, coating completely; lift out and let the excess drain off. Transfer to the cornmeal mixture and toss to coat.

Line a plate with paper towels. When oil is at 350°, begin adding the okra to the oil (do not crowd) and cook about 2 minutes, until golden brown. Remove to paper-towel-lined plate and serve immediately.

GRILLED CORN WITH CHILE-LIME BUTTER

Yield: 12 servings

6 ears of corn

1/2 cup (1 stick) butter, at room temperature

1 tablespoon lime juice

1 tablespoon chopped fresh parsley

2 teaspoons chili powder, or to taste

1 teaspoon garlic powder

1/4 teaspoon salt

1/4 teaspoon freshly ground black pepper

Remove husks and silks from the corn. Place ears in a bowl of cold water for 20 minutes while heating a grill to medium.

In a small bowl, combine the softened butter with the remaining ingredients.

Remove corn from water and shake off excess. Place the ears on the grill. Cook for about 15 minutes, turning every few minutes so that all sides cook evenly. Break each ear in half and stack corn in a large bowl. Spread the seasoned butter over the hot corn and let it melt over the top.

RED, WHITE AND BLUE PIE

This pie is simple, cool and creamy, and the lemon filling combines well with the fresh summer berries. To change the flavor profile, you could use lime or orange juice.

Yield: 8 servings

Single 9-inch piecrust, prebaked according to package instructions and cooled

3 egg yolks, beaten

21 oz. (1 1/2 cans) sweetened condensed milk

1 1/2 cups lemon juice

2 teaspoons pure vanilla extract

1/2 cup whipping cream

2 cups fresh mixed berries

Preheat oven to 350° and have the piecrust ready. In a large bowl, whisk together the egg yolks, sweetened condensed milk, lemon juice and vanilla until thick and creamy. Pour into the piecrust and bake for 20 minutes. Remove from oven and allow to cool; then refrigerate for at least 4 hours.

Just before serving, whip the cream until soft peaks form, spread whipped cream over the top of filling and top with fresh berries.

CHAPTER 6

CAMPFIRE-CHIC COOKOUT: DINNER AND BREAKFAST

MENU

Dinner: *Skillet Honey Cornbread • Cowgirl Stew • Tropical Dump Cake • Mexican Hot Chocolate*
Breakfast: *Chilaquiles Rojo • Chuckwagon Almond Croissants • Campfire Caffe Latte*

For most Texas cowgirls, outdoor cooking is pretty common. Whether it's an evening of grilling or something as simple as campfire hot dogs and s'mores, we've all enjoyed the camaraderie that comes from gathering around the fire, laughing, telling stories and keeping warm. Another form of outdoor cooking that taps into cowgirl history is old-fashioned Dutch oven cookery. In this country it dates all the way back to colonial days; indeed, Paul Revere is commonly credited with designing the flat lid with a ridge around the rim to keep coals in place on top, as well as adding the three legs that allow room for coals under the cast-metal pots. The pioneers and frontiersmen of the American West took these pots along with them, and they're particularly associated with the chuckwagon cookery of the big cattle drives.

Some lucky Texas families have cast-iron Dutch ovens that have been passed down through generations, along with the old recipes. Recent times have seen a revival of interest in Dutch oven cooking, with clubs and competitions devoted to re-creating the campfire cooking and camaraderie of times past. The internet is full of guides offering instruction on everything from how to build a proper fire to how to season a Dutch oven to how to position coals.

Live-coal or charcoal cooking requires a cast-iron pot with three legs, a flat flanged lid (which can also be turned upside-down and placed over coals to cook eggs or flapjacks) and a wire bail handle (modern-day Dutch ovens such as those made by Le Creuset are best reserved for home use). Tools you'll need include long gloves of heavy leather or silicone, a lid-lifter, a small shovel and long tongs for moving the coals. The cooking equipment is easy to find in sporting-goods stores; you can also look for secondhand cast-iron pieces in antiques stores and resale shops.

Planning this Dutch oven cookout with a few fellow cowgirls will require gathering several cast-iron ovens, along with all the gear for mixing and serving. You'll need a reliable cooler, too.

You will also need the essentials for starting a fire. Hickory, oak or pecan wood is preferred, but charcoal briquettes will also work well (bring a chimney starter). Before you head out for your camp, make sure you or one of your cowgirl crew is versed in campfire construction — or that you've a friendly cowboy nearby who'll build you a fire in exchange for a stake in the leftovers.

Doing your recipe prep at home in advance is also helpful. Portion your ingredients, chop the vegetables and store them in individual containers (heavy zip-seal plastic bags are ideal), carefully pack your cooler with everything that will need to stay cold.

This fun menu for an overnight cookout includes recipes for both dinner and breakfast, including some of my favorite comfort-food dishes that work well for either conventional or campfire cooking. In case you're not up for an overnight under the stars, we've included instructions for cooking each recipe in the comfort of your own cozy kitchen.

These are not your typical chuckwagon recipes, but they're just the ticket for modern-day Dutch oven cookery — and perfect for a girls' weekend of glamping in the great outdoors.

DUTCH OVEN TIPS

Once your fire is built, here are a few Dutch oven tips to ensure a successful cookout:

• Let the fire burn down to red-hot coals and smoldering ash before you begin to cook. Smoldering coals will retain heat for about 2 hours. If you'll be cooking for longer, keep some wood on the fire so you can add new coals as the old ones burn out.

• Preheat the oven and lid over the coals before beginning any recipe. For easy cleanup and reuse of the oven, line it with heavy-duty aluminum foil.

• Dutch oven cooking relies on coals being placed under the Dutch oven and on top of the lid; for baking, many Dutch oven experts will tell you, you need more coals on top than on bottom. To reach 350°, the most common baking temperature, use a total of twice as many coals as the diameter of the oven in inches. If you can hold your hand above the open pot, just at rim level, for 5 seconds before having to snatch it away, the temperature inside should be around 350°.

• During cooking, lift the entire oven and rotate it a quarter-turn in the coals every 20 minutes or so, to ensure even heating.

• Surprisingly, it is easier to overcook or burn your food than to undercook it in a Dutch oven. Lift the lid occasionally and check the progress of the cooking at the top and bottom of the oven (lift the lid straight up so that ashes from the lid don't tip into the food). Adjust the temperature as needed by removing or adding coals from the lid or underneath.

SKILLET HONEY CORNBREAD

Yield: 8 slices

1 cup stone-ground yellow cornmeal

1 cup flour

1 tablespoon baking powder

1 teaspoon salt

1/2 cup honey

1 cup whole milk

1 large egg

1/2 cup (1 stick) unsalted butter

CONVENTIONAL METHOD

Preheat oven to 400°. Heat a 12-inch cast-iron skillet in the oven for 15 minutes.

In a large bowl, whisk together cornmeal, flour, baking powder and salt.

If your honey is thick or crystallized, heat a small pan of water to a simmer and remove from heat; place the opened jar of honey in the water and let it sit for 5 minutes; then stir until smooth. (I don't advise microwaving honey.)

Measure 1/2 cup honey into a medium bowl and whisk with milk and egg to blend.

Carefully remove hot skillet from oven and add the butter to it; swirl skillet until butter is melted. Transfer all but 2 tablespoons of the melted butter to the bowl with the milk mixture, reserving the 2 tablespoons in the skillet.

Add milk mixture to cornmeal mixture and stir until just combined. Do not overmix. Pour batter into skillet. Bake until browned around edges and cooked through, about 20 to 25 minutes. Cool in skillet and invert onto platter. Cut into wedges.

CAMPFIRE METHOD

At-home prep: Warm the honey to loosen. Mix the dry ingredients and pack in a zip-close plastic bag.

At the camp: Follow the instructions for conventional method, ensuring that Dutch oven and lid are preheated well over the briquettes or coals.

Pour cornbread batter into Dutch oven and place over 10 to 12 coals. Cover oven and distribute the same number of coals evenly around the lid. Bake for about 30 minutes, or until cornbread is lightly browned on top. Halfway through, rotate pot a half-turn in the coals and check for even cooking. If top is browning too fast, remove some coals from the lid; if the cornbread begins to pull away from the pan before the middle is set, the bottom of the pan is probably too hot; push some coals aside.

COWGIRL STEW

Created with Dutch oven cooking in mind, this stew has become a family favorite at home as well. It has a spicy twist that makes it perfect on a cold winter night, and the amber ale lends a deep, rich flavor.

Yield: 4 to 6 servings

1 1/2 pounds beef stew meat, cut into 1-inch pieces

3 tablespoons barbecue seasoning, divided

1 tablespoon brown sugar

2 slices raw bacon, diced

3 tablespoons flour

1 onion, sliced

2 carrots, finely diced

12-oz. bottle of amber ale

14.5-oz. can diced tomatoes with chipotle peppers

1 cup beef broth

1 cup water

1 cup frozen peas, thawed

Salt and pepper, to taste

CONVENTIONAL METHOD

Place the meat in a large bowl. Add 2 tablespoons of the barbecue rub and the brown sugar. Rub the seasoning into the meat to coat thoroughly and refrigerate for at least 4 hours or overnight.

In a large pot or Dutch oven, sauté the bacon over low heat to render out as much fat as possible without browning. Using a slotted spoon, remove bacon and drain on paper towel. Leave fat in pot.

Turn the heat to high and brown the meat on all sides in the bacon fat. Add the flour, onions and carrots and stir to combine.

Pour in the beer and bring to a boil; boil briskly, uncovered, until reduced by half. Add the tomatoes, broth, water, reserved bacon pieces and remaining tablespoon of barbecue seasoning. Stir to combine and bring back to a boil.

Reduce to a simmer, cover and cook over very low heat for about 1 1/2 hours or until the meat is fork- tender. Watch the liquid level and add more water or broth, if necessary.

Add the peas at the end of the cooking process and stir to warm through. Taste and add salt and pepper to taste. Serve over thick-sliced toasted bread or rice.

CAMPFIRE METHOD

At-home prep: Combine the meat with the seasoning and brown sugar and seal in a plastic bag. Dice bacon; seal in plastic bag. Slice onion and dice carrots; seal tightly in plastic bag. Refrigerate all until time to pack in cooler. Measure out frozen peas into plastic bag; seal and return to freezer until time to pack in cooler.

At the camp: Preheat Dutch oven and lid. Place 16 coals or briquettes underneath pot for high heat. As the pot is heating up, sauté the bacon to render the fat without browning the bacon and remove as above to drain. Add meat and brown over high heat. Stir in the flour until thoroughly combined, then add the vegetables and liquid and bring to a boil.

Cover pot; remove 6 coals from underneath the oven and place on top of the lid. Check after 10 minutes to ensure liquid is simmering but not boiling; remove or add coals as necessary. Continue to check progress occasionally and add more water or broth if necessary. You may need to add more coals as the original ones burn down, so keep some wood on the fire to supply the new coals. Cook for about 2 hours, or until meat is fork-tender, rotating oven a quarter-turn every 30 minutes.

TROPICAL DUMP CAKE

Yield: 10 servings

2 (20-oz.) cans crushed pineapple
18.25-oz. box yellow cake mix
1/2 cup (1 stick) unsalted butter, cut into tablespoons
2 cups chopped pecans
1 cup sweetened coconut flakes
Vanilla ice cream, for serving

CONVENTIONAL METHOD

Preheat oven to 350°. Lightly grease a 9-by-13-inch baking pan.

Drain 1 can of the pineapple, discarding syrup, but leave other can undrained. Empty both cans of pineapple into baking pan and spread pineapple evenly over bottom.

Sprinkle cake mix over top of fruit. Dot evenly with butter and sprinkle with pecans and coconut flakes. Bake at 350° for 45 to 50 minutes, or until golden and cooked through.

CAMPFIRE METHOD

Line a 12-inch Dutch oven with heavy-duty foil and preheat the oven and lid. Add cake ingredients, following conventional instructions. Place over 10 to 12 coals or briquettes. Cover and place the same number of coals on the lid.

Bake for 45 to 60 minutes. About halfway through, rotate oven a half-turn and check cake for even cooking. If top is browning too fast, remove coals from the lid; if bottom is browning too fast, push some coals aside to cool the fire.

MEXICAN HOT CHOCOLATE

Can be spiked with brandy, Irish cream or chocolate liqueur.

Yield: 6 servings

1/4 cup cocoa powder

1/4 cup sugar

2 teaspoons pure vanilla extract

2 teaspoons cinnamon

1/8 teaspoon cayenne pepper

2 (12-oz.) cans evaporated milk

2 cups water

In a small bowl, stir together cocoa powder, sugar, vanilla, cinnamon and cayenne pepper (for the camp-out, this can be mixed at home and sealed in a plastic bag). Add evaporated milk and water to a saucepan over medium heat. When milk mixture starts to steam, begin whisking in the cocoa mixture until all ingredients are incorporated. Cover and bring just to a simmer; serve immediately.

CHILAQUILES ROJO

At home, this recipe is great for weekend breakfast or anytime you have houseguests. It's easy, quick and a delicious alternative to traditional breakfast casseroles.

Yield: 6 servings

14.5-oz. can diced tomatoes, drained
2 cups prepared pico de gallo (see note)
1 cup water
6 cups tortilla chips
6 eggs
3/4 cup grated Cheddar cheese
1/4 cup chopped cilantro
1/2 cup sour cream, for garnish

CONVENTIONAL METHOD

Make tomato sauce: In a blender, combine the diced tomatoes, pico de gallo and water. Blend until creamy.

Place the chips in a 10-inch cast-iron skillet. Cover with the tomato sauce and bring to a boil; then turn heat to low. Crack one egg at a time into the skillet, taking care to keep yolks intact and distributing eggs evenly around the pan with some space in between.

Cover the skillet and cook over low heat for about 12 minutes. Sprinkle 2 tablespoons of cheese over each egg and sprinkle with cilantro. Cover again and cook an additional 3 minutes, or until cheese is melted. Pass sour cream to garnish.

NOTE: Prepared pico de gallo (a fresh relish/salsa usually comprising finely chopped jalapeno or serrano chiles, tomatoes, cilantro and lime juice) can be found in the refrigerated section of most grocery-store produce departments.

CAMPFIRE METHOD

At-home prep: Blend tomatoes, pico de gallo and water; seal in a plastic bag and pack in cooler. Grate cheese and chop cilantro; pack separately for cooler.

Preheat Dutch oven. Place over 8 to 10 coals or briquettes. Per instructions for conventional method, add chips and tomato sauce and bring to a boil; then remove a few coals from underneath to reduce heat. Add eggs as above and cover pot. Cook for about 10 minutes, checking after about 8 minutes. When eggs are just starting to set, add the cheese and cilantro; replace lid and cook for 3 to 5 minutes more, until cheese is melted. Pass sour cream to garnish.

CHUCKWAGON ALMOND CROISSANTS

Yield: 16 croissants

7 oz. tube almond paste (see note)

6 tablespoons (3/4 stick) room-temperature butter

3 tablespoons sugar

1 tablespoon cinnamon

1 tablespoon flour

2 (8-oz.) packages refrigerated crescent-roll dough

CONVENTIONAL METHOD

Preheat oven to 350°. Line a baking sheet with parchment.

Make the almond filling: Into a medium-sized mixing bowl, grate or finely crumble the almond paste. Add the butter, sugar, cinnamon and flour and mash together with a fork until well combined.

Unroll crescent dough into triangles. Spread almond filling down the middle of each triangle. Roll dough toward the point of the triangle. Place on baking sheet and curve into crescent shape. Bake for 14 to 16 minutes, or until puffed and golden.

NOTE: Almond paste can usually be found in the grocery-store baking section.

CAMPFIRE METHOD

Line a Dutch oven with heavy-duty foil. Preheat oven and lid. Make crescents as instructed above.

Place crescents in the bottom of the oven, packing tightly into a circular pattern around the perimeter of the oven and then filling in the center.

Place pot over 10 to 12 coals. Cover and place the same number of coals on the lid. Cook about 20 minutes, or until dough is cooked through and croissants are golden, checking halfway through for even cooking.

CAMPFIRE CAFFE LATTE

Try this recipe anytime you want to make quick homemade lattes.

Yield: 6 servings

3 cups whole milk

2 cups water

6 teaspoons instant coffee

Granulated sugar, if desired

Combine all ingredients in a saucepan over medium heat; cover and bring just to a simmer. Stir until all ingredients are combined and the coffee granules and sugar are dissolved. Serve immediately.

CHAPTER 7
FIESTA ON THE FARM

MENU

Mexican Paloma • Garden-Fresh Guacamole • Watermelon Salsa •
Classic Tex-Mex Beef & Cheese Enchiladas • Refried Black Beans •
Spicy Mexican Rice • Sopapilla Cheesecake Cookies

For the tried-and-true cowgirl on a farm or ranch, living on the land is
a lot of work. The list of daily chores is endless: animals to take care of,
crops and a kitchen garden to tend to, the land to look after, the hands
to take care of. And that's just outside.

Feeding those hungry cowboys can be a major feat, but it can also be a
lot of fun. After all the hard work they do, cowboys — and cowgirls —
need time to relax and celebrate, and what better way than with every
Texan's favorite cuisine? I'm speaking, of course, of Mexican food.

To be perfectly honest, I don't think any Texan can go more than a
week without indulging in south-of-the-border fare. Mexican food
has a uniquely cherished place in Texas, and a good measure of ranch
cooking has woven itself into Mexican culinary traditions to produce
the hybrid known in these parts as Tex-Mex. As a cuisine, "Tex-Mex" is
hard to define, but whatever it is, we can't live without it.

Fortunately, Mexican food is one restaurant cuisine that's easy to
prepare at home, and most of the recipes can easily be doubled or
tripled to feed a crowd. The recipes here also incorporate lots of fresh
garden vegetables and herbs that are staples in Texas gardens.

For this fiesta, keep the table fun and unfussy. A mix of colors creates a vibrant table, and I love the classic Fiestaware for this type of event. (I have a friend who was given her vintage set by a certified old-time cowgirl from a South Texas ranching family who used her Fiestaware only when she cooked Mexican food.) For a less fragile dinnerware choice, shop the party store for a colorful variety of plastic plates and bowls; pick bold hues of red, green, yellow, blue or orange.

Mexican horse blankets are a natural choice to cover the tabletop, and small potted cactus plants or succulents lined up down the center of the table add a nice touch. For crafty table accents, hit a Mexican import or craft store to find punched-metal lanterns or fun little ceramic figures, which can be picked up cheaply enough to be used at each place setting for guests to take home. If you're having your fiesta outside, some piñatas hanging from the patio eaves or low-hanging branches are a fun addition. Chile-shaped string lights are easy to find, too, and more punched-metal lanterns will cast an enchanting pattern of light over the proceeds.

Each of these recipes can be made in advance and easily reheated. That's important to a cowgirl, because days on the farm are long, and sometimes you have to wait for the sun to set and the cows to come home before the dinner bell rings.

MEXICAN PALOMA

The margarita may be the most popular Mexican drink in America, but if you're in Mexico it's the paloma — a more refreshing beverage of choice on a hot summer day.

Yield: 1 cocktail

1/4 cup tequila
1/3 cup grapefruit juice
1/3 cup sparkling water
Juice of 1/2 lime
Lime wedge for garnish

Add ice to a tall glass. Pour in tequila, grapefruit juice, sparkling water and lime juice. Stir gently, then serve with lime-wedge garnish.

GARDEN-FRESH GUACAMOLE

Though it's possible to grow avocados in Texas, and some people do, generally we get our avocados from our neighbors across the border. Ditto with limes, but the other ingredients in this recipe are typically found in a cowgirl's vegetable garden. Being from East Texas, the onions I prefer to use in summer are the sweet Noonday onions, grown only within a 10-mile radius of the city of Noonday. They're a close relative to the 1015 Texas Super Sweet Onion, but if you ask a cowgirl from Noonday, she'll tell you that there's magic in that sandy soil and that no other onion compares.

Yield: About 5 cups

4 large ripe avocados, peel and seed discarded

Juice of 1 large lime (about 1/4 cup), plus a lime wedge for garnish

1/2 small sweet onion, diced small

1 medium tomato, seeded and diced small

1 jalapeño, cored, seeded and finely diced

1/4 cup finely minced fresh cilantro leaves, plus a sprig for garnish

1/2 teaspoon salt

1/2 teaspoon black pepper

In a large, shallow bowl, mash the avocado flesh with the lime juice. Stir in the onion, tomato, jalapeño, cilantro, salt and pepper. Transfer to a serving dish.

This can be made an hour in advance; press plastic wrap onto the surface of the guacamole to prevent browning and place in the refrigerator. When ready to serve, garnish with a sprig of cilantro in the middle and a lime wedge atop the cilantro.

WATERMELON SALSA

There are three ingredients that are essential when it comes to surviving a sweltering Texas summer – watermelon, cucumber and mint. Just the thought of them seems to lower the temperature. When you scoop up this salsa, you get that refreshing trinity of cool flavor, plus heat from the jalapeño, the sweetness of summer peaches and local honey and a little kick from the onion. (You can use the sweet Noonday or 1015 onions, of course, but I like red onions here because they add a punch of color.) This light and colorful salsa is equally refreshing as a dip with chips or as a relish to dollop over grilled chicken or fish or to garnish seafood tacos.

Yield: About 4 cups

2 cups ripe watermelon flesh, cut into 1/4-inch cubes

1 large tomato, seeded and diced small

1 peach, peeled, pitted and diced small

1/2 medium red onion, finely diced

1/2 small cucumber, peeled, seeded and diced small

1 jalapeño, cored, seeded and finely diced

2 tablespoons finely chopped fresh mint leaves

2 tablespoons finely chopped fresh cilantro

1 tablespoon honey (see note)

Combine all ingredients in a large bowl and chill for up to an hour; stir and strain before serving to remove excess liquid.

NOTE: If your honey is thick or crystallized, heat a small pan of water to a simmer and remove from heat. Place the jar of honey in the warm water and let it sit for 5 minutes; then stir until smooth. (I don't advise microwaving honey.)

CLASSIC TEX-MEX BEEF & CHEESE ENCHILADAS

Growing up, I loved my mother's enchiladas; none could compare to hers. After I left for college, the craving for her enchiladas grew and I asked her for the recipe. She handed me a packet of enchilada sauce mix and told me to read the back. Really? Eventually I created my own sauce recipe with a very similar flavor. It's as easy as the packet, and you can adjust the seasonings to your taste.

Yield: 10 enchiladas

1 pound lean ground beef

2 teaspoons cornstarch

1 tablespoon sweet paprika

1 tablespoon ground cumin

1 tablespoon chili powder

1 tablespoon cocoa powder

1 tablespoon black pepper

1/2 teaspoon salt

1/2 teaspoon garlic powder

1 tablespoon canola oil

1 medium yellow onion, diced small

2 cups low-sodium canned tomato sauce

2 cups vegetable or chicken stock

2 cups shredded Mexican-style cheese

1 package flour tortillas (10- or 12-count)

Brown the ground beef in a skillet over medium heat, drain off any excess fat and set aside to cool.

In a small bowl, stir together the cornstarch with all the seasonings, combining thoroughly. Set aside.

To make the sauce, in a saucepot, heat the oil over medium heat and sauté the onion until soft. Pour in the tomato sauce and add the cornstarch-spice mix, stirring until spices are completely incorporated. Pour in the stock and stir to combine. Bring to a boil and let simmer, uncovered, for 5 minutes to thicken. Remove from heat and set aside to cool before assembling enchiladas.

When ready to cook, preheat oven to 375°.

Measure out a cup of the sauce and a cup of the cheese and set aside to top the enchiladas.

Stir a cup of the remaining sauce into the ground beef; then spread another cup of the sauce in the bottom of a 9-by-13-inch baking dish.

To assemble the enchiladas, spoon a couple of tablespoons of the ground-beef mixture down the center of a tortilla; add a generous sprinkle of cheese and a spoonful of sauce. Do not overfill. Roll up the tortilla tightly and place seam side down in the baking dish. Repeat until you run out of ingredients; the enchiladas should fill the pan snugly. If you have sauce or cheese left over, just add it to what you have reserved for the topping.

After rolling all the enchiladas, cover them thoroughly with the reserved sauce and sprinkle the reserved cheese evenly on top. Cover with foil and bake for 30 minutes; then remove foil and return to oven to bake for a few more minutes uncovered. Serve immediately.

These can be made the night before and kept in the refrigerator until ready to bake, or they can be frozen for longer. To freeze, cover the pan tightly with foil; to cook, remove pan from freezer and let thaw overnight in the refrigerator, then bring to room temperature for 30 minutes to 1 hour. Bake, still covered with foil, in a preheated 325-degree oven (note the lower temperature) for 45 minutes; then remove foil and bake for an additional 15 minutes. Check for doneness and bake longer if necessary, until enchiladas are heated through, sauce is bubbling and cheese is melted.

REFRIED BLACK BEANS

Yield: 4 to 6 servings

3 tablespoons canola oil

1 medium yellow onion, diced small

2 cloves garlic, finely minced

2 (15-oz.) cans whole black beans, drained and rinsed

1/2 cup tomato-based salsa, homemade or purchased

1/2 teaspoon chili powder

1/2 teaspoon salt

1/2 teaspoon black pepper

Chopped fresh cilantro, sour cream and pico de gallo, to garnish

Over medium heat, add oil to a medium saucepan. Add diced onion and sauté, stirring frequently, until softened, about 2 minutes. Add minced garlic and sauté, stirring frequently, for an additional minute, taking care not to burn the garlic.

Remove pan from heat and add the drained black beans; stir to blend. Mash bean mixture coarsely with a potato masher, leaving some of the beans whole to keep a chunky texture.

Stir in the salsa, chili powder, salt and pepper; return to medium-low heat and cook, uncovered, stirring occasionally, until heated through. Garnish with cilantro, sour cream and pico de gallo.

SPICY MEXICAN RICE

Yield: 6 servings

2 tablespoons canola oil

1/2 yellow onion, diced small

2 cloves garlic, finely minced

2 cups long-grain rice

10-oz. can Ro-Tel diced tomatoes and green chilies, drained

8-oz. can tomato sauce

2 cups chicken or vegetable broth

1 cup corn kernels, fresh if possible, frozen if out of season

1/4 cup chopped fresh cilantro

Salt and pepper to taste

In a large skillet, heat oil over medium heat. Add diced onion and sauté, stirring frequently, until softened, about 2 minutes. Add the minced garlic and sauté, stirring frequently, for a minute, taking care not to burn. Add the rice and stir continuously until rice is slightly toasted and fragrant, about a minute.

Pour in the Ro-Tel, the tomato sauce and the broth. Stir to combine and bring to a simmer. Cover and turn heat to low. Let simmer for about 15 minutes, checking the liquid occasionally and adding water in small amounts if needed.

When rice is tender and grains are separate, fluff with a fork and gently stir in the corn and cilantro. Taste for seasoning and add salt and pepper to taste.

SOPAPILLA CHEESECAKE COOKIES

Mexican-restaurant sopapillas are difficult to duplicate at home, but these flaky cookies are almost as good and can be made a day in advance. The secret is purchased puff pastry dough.

Yield: 30 cookies

8 ounces cream cheese, at room temperature

1/2 cup sugar, plus extra for sprinkling

1 tablespoon powdered cinnamon, plus extra for sprinkling

Flour for working with pastry

2 sheets purchased frozen puff pastry, thawed according to package directions

1/2 cup chopped pecans, divided

2 tablespoons honey, divided, plus more for serving

Preheat oven to 400°.

In a bowl, stir together the softened cream cheese, sugar and cinnamon, mixing until thoroughly combined. Set aside.

Flour a clean work surface, a rolling pin and a baking sheet. Unfold one of the pastry sheets onto the work surface and roll out slightly to smooth.

Using a spatula, spread half the cream cheese mixture over the pastry. Top with half the pecans and drizzle with a tablespoon of honey. Roll up the dough like a jelly roll and carefully transfer the roll of dough onto the floured baking sheet. Repeat with the other sheet of puff pastry.

Place the baking sheet with the rolls of dough, uncovered, in the freezer for 30 minutes. Remove and slice rolls crossways into 1/2-inch slices; you should have about 15 slices. Evenly space the slices, flat sides down, on 2 baking sheets. Sprinkle each with additional sugar and cinnamon.

Bake for 15 minutes, or until pastries are golden. Remove the pastries from the baking sheets and cool on a rack for 10 minutes. Store at room temperature.

To serve, drizzle pastries with additional honey.

CHAPTER 8
GULF COAST SUNSET SOIREE

MENU

Peach Mojitos • Strawberry-Melon Coolers • Crawfish-and-Cornbread-Stuffed Mushrooms • Fried-Oyster Sliders With Spicy Lime Mayonnaise • Shrimp Tostadas With Grapefruit Salsa • Texas Gulf Coast Crab Boil

When you think of a cowgirl, you probably don't picture her on the beach, but South Texas' Gulf Coast is actually the cradle of Texas ranching.

Long before Texas' cattle industry shifted northward, the state's first cattle drives saw ranchers in Southeast Texas herding their stock to New Orleans' markets. In the Coastal Bend, Spanish land grants were the genesis of cattle empires such as the legendary King and Kenedy ranches.

And on many of those ranches, freshly caught seafood was as welcome on the table as beef.

As a young cowgirl I spent a few blissful summers on Matagorda Bay, fishing and crabbing from piers and bridges on the Intracoastal Canal between the Texas mainland and the Gulf of Mexico. We would drive south out of Wharton on Highway 60, down through Bay City and into Matagorda until we started to see water.

I still remember the fun we had during those summers, and crabbing was one of the best parts. Our bait was raw chicken, the neck and other bony parts my mom didn't bother to cook. We'd tie a piece to a long length of twine and lower it into the water. When we felt a tug, it was time to raise the line until the crab came into view just below the surface of the water, where we'd fish it out with a net. We'd keep our catch alive in a mesh bucket floating under the dock while we played on the beach, then pack the crabs in a cooler for the trip home. Once home, I could hardly wait for one of my favorite meals – boiled shell-on crabs with corn and potatoes.

For this party, the crabs are the main attraction, but there are plenty of other Gulf Coast delights to round out the menu. The feast is best served outside on a picnic table spread with newspapers or butcher paper. No need for plates: This is a hands-on, pick-it-up-and-eat-it menu. The crabs and shrimp can be spread down the middle of the table for easy grabbing, with the bowl of potatoes and corn as the centerpiece.

Fill small galvanized buckets with colorful napkins, seafood mallets, nutcrackers and picks. More buckets can be turned upside down to use as stands for the plates of stuffed mushrooms, oyster sliders and shrimp tostadas. If you like to dunk your crab into melted butter, look for tiny versions of the galvanized buckets at craft stores and use them as individual containers for dipping. To hold the discard shells, set out larger buckets. When everyone is finished digging in, pass around a decorative bowl filled with wet wipes.

You can do the crab boil indoors, too: Simply drain the boiled crabs and shrimp well and pile them in large serving bowls or deep platters. Be sure to supply plenty of napkins, and maybe seafood bibs, found at party or kitchen stores.

PEACH MOJITOS

My favorite mojitos come from a restaurant in Tyler, Texas, called Villa Montez. Cool, refreshing, not too sweet, they come in a variety of flavors. I wish I could replicate them, but until owners Carlos and Mundo give up their secret recipe, I will have to settle for my own version of this popular Cuban cocktail. In summertime, when peaches are fresh and delicious, I like to make a peach mojito.

Yield: 4 cocktails

2 ripe peaches, peeled and cut into wedges

20 fresh mint leaves

1 1/2 tablespoons turbinado (raw) sugar (see note)

1/2 cup white rum

1/3 cup lime juice

Club soda

Lime wedges for garnish

Fill 4 glasses with ice.

In a blender, puree the peaches. Set aside.

Add the mint leaves and sugar to a cocktail shaker and muddle to release the flavor of the mint. Add the pureed peaches, rum and lime juice to the shaker with about 1/2 cup ice cubes. Shake for 10 seconds and strain evenly into ice-filled glasses. Top each glass with a splash of club soda and garnish with a lime wedge.

NOTE: Turbinado or raw sugar is minimally processed sugar with some natural molasses remaining. It has distinct light-golden-brown crystals and can generally be found with the other varieties of sugar in the grocery store's baking aisle.

STRAWBERRY-MELON COOLERS

On a hot summer day, nothing is more refreshing than a watermelon beverage. This recipe has lots of great flavor without the addition of sugar. You can make two batches — one with sparkling wine, one with sparkling water — if you have kids or those who prefer non-alcoholic drinks among your guests.

Yield: 4 servings

2 cups roughly cubed watermelon
1 cup strawberries, hulled
Juice of 1 lemon
2 cups sparkling water or sparkling wine such as cava or prosecco
Lemon wedges for garnish
Fill 4 tall glasses with ice.

In a blender, combine watermelon, strawberries and lemon juice and puree. Strain puree into a 1-quart pitcher. Add sparkling water or wine; stir well to blend and pour into ice-filled glasses. Garnish with lemon wedges.

CRAWFISH-AND-CORNBREAD-STUFFED MUSHROOMS

I love crawfish, but they are a lot of work, so I buy the frozen tail meat and save myself hours of peeling. Stuffed mushrooms are always requested at my parties, and this crawfish version is a family favorite.

Yield: About 20 mushrooms

1 pound medium-sized white button or cremini mushrooms
1 tablespoon vegetable oil

3 cloves garlic, minced

2 shallots, minced

1/4 cup lemon juice

1 cup packaged cornbread stuffing mix

1/2 cup chicken broth

1/2 pound crawfish tails, roughly chopped

1/2 cup grated Parmesan cheese

1/4 cup chopped fresh Italian parsley

1/2 teaspoon cayenne pepper

1/2 teaspoon black pepper

1/4 teaspoon salt

Clean mushrooms with a damp paper towel; twist out stems and set aside. With a melon baller or small spoon, hollow out the cavities of the mushrooms, reserving the scraps, to allow more room for stuffing. Finely chop the stems and scraps and set aside for the stuffing.

In a large sauté pan, heat oil over medium heat. Add garlic, shallots and chopped mushroom stems and sauté, stirring, for 2 to 3 minutes, until softened. Add the lemon juice and stir and scrape to deglaze the pan. Stir in the cornbread stuffing and the broth. Add the crawfish and remove from heat; then gently stir in the remaining ingredients.

Line a baking sheet with foil and grease the foil with a little vegetable oil. Place the mushroom caps, cavity up, spaced evenly on the baking sheet. Spoon stuffing into mushroom caps, packing tightly. (Mushrooms can be stuffed a day ahead of time; cover with foil and refrigerate.)

When ready to cook, preheat oven to 350°. Bake mushrooms, uncovered, until heated through, about 15 to 20 minutes.

FRIED-OYSTER SLIDERS
WITH SPICY LIME MAYONNAISE

Seek out the largest oysters you can find for these appetizers. Anyone who's spent time in New Orleans will recognize them as oyster po'boys, undressed and given a contemporary remake as cute little sliders. If you like, you can add slivered napa cabbage to the sandwiches for even more crunch.

Yield: 8 sliders

1/2 cup mayonnaise

1 tablespoon freshly squeezed lime juice

1 tablespoon sriracha sauce

8 slider buns

Cooking oil for frying

1 cup flour

1 tablespoon Old Bay seasoning

3 eggs

1 cup panko breadcrumbs (see note)

8 large oysters, shucked

To make the spicy mayonnaise, combine the mayonnaise, lime juice and sriracha. Spread onto the inner surface of each bun half and set buns aside.

In a deep skillet, heat 2 inches of cooking oil over high heat. Set out three shallow bowls for breading the oysters. In the first bowl, stir together the flour and Old Bay seasoning. In the second bowl, thoroughly beat the eggs. In the third bowl, spread a layer of panko breadcrumbs.

When a bit of flour dropped into the oil sizzles immediately and furiously, the oil is hot enough. Dredge each oyster in the flour, shaking off the excess; dip oyster into the beaten eggs and then into the panko to coat thoroughly. Gently slide the oysters into the oil and fry 2 to 3 minutes, or until golden. Do not crowd the skillet, or the oil will cool down; cook in two batches if necessary. Drain fried oysters briefly on a plate lined with paper towels before adding an oyster to each bun.

NOTE: Panko, a Japanese style of breadcrumb with large, light and airy flakes that fry up very crisp, has become mainstream and is available at most larger supermarkets as well as Asian specialty stores.

SHRIMP TOSTADAS WITH GRAPEFRUIT SALSA

Ruby Red grapefruit and Texas Gulf Coast shrimp are two of Texas' most valuable commodities. This recipe combines the two and offers a delicious balance between sweet and spicy.

Yield: 4 tostadas

SALSA

1 orange, peeled, sectioned and chopped

1 grapefruit, peeled, sectioned and chopped

1 cup chopped fresh pineapple

1 tomato, seeded and chopped

1 fresh jalapeño pepper, seeded and finely chopped

2 tablespoons thinly sliced green onion

1 tablespoon chopped fresh cilantro

1/4 teaspoon salt

TACOS

Juice of 1 grapefruit (about 1/2 cup)
2 cloves garlic, minced
2 tablespoons honey
1 tablespoon olive oil
1/2 teaspoon salt
1/4 teaspoon black pepper
16 large shrimp, peeled, deveined, end tail segments removed
4 crunchy tostadas
1 cup shredded cabbage

SALSA

In a serving bowl, stir together all salsa ingredients to combine. Chill for at least 4 hours.

TACOS

In a bowl large enough to hold all the shrimp, make a marinade by whisking together the grapefruit juice, garlic, honey, olive oil, salt and pepper. Add the shrimp and stir well to coat with the marinade. Set bowl in the refrigerator to marinate for 20 minutes.

Meanwhile, arrange the tostadas on a large plate and top each with 1/4 cup cabbage.

Heat a large sauté pan over medium heat. Pour in the shrimp and the marinade and cook, stirring constantly, until shrimp are pink and tails have curled, about 2 to 3 minutes. Remove from heat and divide shrimp among the tostadas, 4 to each. Top each tostada with a spoon of salsa. Serve immediately, passing the remaining salsa alongside.

TEXAS GULF COAST CRAB BOIL

If you have the opportunity to catch your own crabs for this recipe, it is well worth the effort. On the Texas Gulf Coast you will primarily find blue crab, which has delicious meat in the claws and legs. Crabbers are allowed to keep crabs whose body span is 5 inches or more, but anything smaller, as well as any female crab with an egg sac — a disc that resembles a sponge attached to the underside of the body — should be thrown back.

To purchase crabs, go to a seafood market or your supermarket fish counter; you may need to order them in advance of your party. Make sure you have a pot large enough for the boil — you'll need one with a 12- to 15-quart capacity.

Yield: 4 to 6 servings

4 tablespoons Old Bay seasoning

3 lemons, halved, plus lemon wedges for serving

3 pounds small to medium red potatoes, quartered

4 ears corn, husked, silk removed, cut into thirds

8 large crabs

3 dozen large shrimp, raw, shells on

Fill a 12- to 15-quart stockpot 3/4 full with water. Add the seasoning, the 6 lemon halves and the potatoes, cover and bring to a boil. Uncover and let boil for 5 minutes before adding the corn and crabs. (If the crabs are still alive when they go into the pot, place a tight-fitting lid on top of the pot and hold the lid in place with a potholder for about a minute.)

Boil for 5 minutes and then add shrimp. Watch closely; as soon as the shrimp are pink, remove with tongs; when the crabs are bright red, remove with tongs. Transfer the crabs and shrimp to a large bowl.

Remove potatoes and corn with large sieve or slotted spoon and pile in another large bowl. Serve immediately.

CHAPTER 9
FARM-TO-TABLE DINNER PARTY

MENU

Strawberry-Lime Gin and Tonic • Peach Iced Tea • Heirloom Tomato Salsa • Rosemary-Grilled Lamb Chops With Fresh Mint Sauce • Garden Tomato Platter With Fresh Herbs • Marinated Summer Squash Salad • Crispy New Potatoes With Goat Cheese • Grilled Pound Cake With Blackberries and Lemon Cream

"Farm-to-table" is a phrase that's been trending mightily in recent years. Farm-to-table menus are the draw at the hippest restaurants, whose chefs forge partnerships with farmers and whose menus tell us which local growers we should thank for the turnips or the tomatoes. We read articles and hear commentary extolling the importance of local produce and encouraging us to eat seasonally and to source products with minimal environmental impact.

For a Texas country cowgirl, there's nothing trendy about all this. It's a way of life, practiced for generations, that simply means living off the land, eating what you or neighboring farmers have grown – plant or animal – and tending to crops year 'round to ensure a profitable harvest. Those who are part of this tradition have a big head start on the farm-to-table trend.

City cowgirls have tapped into the tradition too, as the farm-to-table model has spawned a growing crowd of urbanites who support local farmers, ranchers and food artisans. Farmer's markets have never been more popular, and more and more farms are offering CSAs (community-supported agriculture), whereby members get weekly boxes of whatever produce is being harvested. As each season brings new crops — along with the last hurrah for the previous season's bounty — planning a dinner party around whatever is fresh from the market or the backyard garden is a joyful way to celebrate the season.

As spring unfolds and summer draws nearer, we daydream about the first bites of the season: leafy greens, juicy peaches, succulent berries, fat homegrown tomatoes, fresh herbs. Soon come sweet onions, lush melons, hand-shelled field peas, plump-kerneled sweet corn and, eventually, more zucchini than any one cowgirl could handle. It's a time of year when our cup runneth over, and it's a joy to share the bounty.

When fruits and vegetables are in season, at their peak and fresh from the field, their intense flavors make cooking easy. Each recipe in this menu is designed to highlight those peak flavors, with simple seasoning and cooking techniques.

A celebration of early-summer flavor wouldn't be complete without the colorful wildflowers that grow in fields, gardens and roadsides across Texas. The décor for your farm-to-table dinner can be as natural and seasonal as your ingredients: Gather wildflowers for cheery multicolor bouquets, or purchase them at your local farmers' market. Accent the flowers with fresh herbs and arrange them in plastic glasses that will fit into new clay flowerpots. You might experiment with using foliage from whatever's going great guns in your garden — curly tendriled pea vines, maybe — or fragrant fresh herbs.

Burlap fabric for runners and place mats can be found at craft or fabric stores; pick up some wide grosgrain ribbon and iron-on adhesive tape so you can add colorful borders to your rustic DIY table linens.

STRAWBERRY-LIME GIN AND TONIC

Yield: 2 cocktails

4 strawberries, stemmed and sliced

1 lime

3 oz. gin

12 oz. tonic water

Place the strawberries in the bottom of a cocktail shaker and muddle them to break them up and release their juice. Add ice cubes to fill shaker about half full. Cut the lime in half; squeeze juice from one half into the shaker and slice the other half into wedges or wheels for garnish. Add gin to the shaker and shake for 10 seconds.

Fill two tall glasses with ice and strain the cocktail into the glasses, dividing equally. Top with tonic water and garnish with lime wedges.

PEACH ICED TEA

Yield: 9 cups

1 family-size tea bag, or 4 individual tea bags

2 quarts water

3 fresh peaches

Fresh mint sprigs for garnish

Brew the iced tea in the water according to your favorite method.

Pit, peel and slice two of the peaches and puree in a food processor. Cut the third peach (you can leave it unpeeled) into thin slices and set aside to use as garnish.

Add peach puree to the tea, stir to combine and chill for at least 2 hours or overnight. After chilling, strain the tea through a fine-mesh sieve into a pitcher and discard the solids.

Place ice in glasses and pour tea over the ice. Garnish with mint sprigs and peach slices.

HEIRLOOM TOMATO SALSA

Nothing says summer like the taste of fresh garden tomatoes. I can't wait for the first batch each year. They're what makes this salsa so good. I like to use Fresno peppers or red jalapeños. They have a different type of heat and a deeper, less grassy flavor than the usual green jalapeños.

Yield: 4 cups

2 pounds heirloom tomatoes, mixed varieties

1 Texas sweet onion

1 to 2 large Fresno peppers or red jalapeños, seeds and ribs removed, minced

1/4 cup chopped fresh cilantro

1/4 cup freshly squeezed lime juice

1 teaspoon coarse salt

1/2 teaspoon freshly ground pepper

Cut the tomatoes in half equatorially, seed them, cut them into medium dice and place in a serving bowl.

Peel the onion and cut it into small dice; rinse the dice with hot water in a fine-mesh sieve for 30 seconds. Shake off excess water and add onion dice to the bowl.

Add remaining ingredients to bowl and mix gently. Cover and chill for 30 minutes to allow flavors to combine. Serve as an hors d'oeuvre with chips.

ROSEMARY-GRILLED LAMB CHOPS WITH FRESH MINT SAUCE

Spring is the traditional season for lamb, whose production is on the rise in Texas. After the drought of 2011, many cattle ranchers made the switch to sheep, which require less maintenance, food and acreage. I am fortunate to live down the road from a lamb rancher, so I frequently enjoy lamb prepared different ways. It cooks just like beef, but it shouldn't be cooked past medium doneness. When cooked to well-done, the meat toughens and takes on a gamey flavor.

The refreshing spark of mint is a traditional foil for lamb's rich flavor; once you've made mint sauce from garden-fresh leaves, you'll never go back to mint jelly's pale imitation.

Yield: 4 servings

LAMB CHOPS

2 tablespoons vegetable oil

2 garlic cloves, finely chopped

2 tablespoons finely chopped fresh rosemary needles

1 teaspoon coarse sea salt

1 teaspoon ground black pepper

12 lamb chops, 1 to 1 1/2 inches thick

MINT SAUCE

1 cup loosely packed fresh mint leaves

2 teaspoons sugar

2 tablespoons very hot water

1/4 cup malt vinegar

LAMB CHOPS

Heat a grill or grill pan over high heat.

In a small bowl, combine the oil, garlic, rosemary, salt and pepper. Rub this mixture onto both sides of the lamb chops. Place lamb chops on the grill and cook about 3 to 4 minutes on each side, to medium-rare. Remove chops to a warmed serving platter, tent them with foil and allow them to rest for about 5 minutes, while you make the mint sauce.

MINT SAUCE

Pile the mint leaves on a cutting board. Sprinkle the sugar evenly over the mint and chop into a fine paste. Scrape the paste into a small bowl; pour the hot water over it and allow to steep for a couple of minutes. Add the vinegar, stir well and transfer to a sauceboat to serve alongside the lamb.

GARDEN TOMATO PLATTER WITH FRESH HERBS

When you have sweet, ripe tomatoes fresh from the garden, they don't need gilding, and this is as simple as it gets: Slice your tomatoes about a quarter-inch thick and overlap them in concentric circles or in a spiral on a platter. Drizzle with a little good olive oil (and a scant splash of sherry vinegar, if you like); sprinkle evenly with a pinch of flaky sea salt such as Maldon and a generous grinding of coarse black pepper. Using basil, Italian parsley, mint or a mixture, scatter chopped or torn herbs generously atop. This is particularly striking with multi-colored heirloom tomatoes.

MARINATED SUMMER SQUASH SALAD

This is a salad I learned to make in Southern Italy, where almost every recipe includes lemon. Marinating the squash in lemon brightens and sharpens all its natural flavors. The citrus marinade also tenderizes the squash a bit, but it's still best to start with small young squashes, recently picked; they'll have the most delicate texture, and negligible seeds, for eating raw. If you have a spiral vegetable slicer, you can cut the squash into noodle-like strands for a whimsical and colorful presentation.

Yield: 4 to 6 servings

2 small yellow summer squash

2 small zucchini

Juice and zest of 1 large lemon

1/2 teaspoon crushed red-pepper flakes

1 tablespoon extra-virgin olive oil

1 teaspoon white-wine vinegar

1/4 teaspoon salt

1/4 teaspoon freshly ground black pepper

Cut the ends off the squashes and discard. Shaving lengthwise with a swivel peeler, remove the top layer of skin and discard.

Using the swivel peeler or a mandoline, shave very thin ribbon-like lengthwise slices of the squash flesh into a medium bowl. Add the lemon juice and zest and mix well. Briefly chop the crushed red-pepper flakes and add to the bowl. Add all remaining ingredients and toss well.

Refrigerate for at least 30 minutes. Serve cold as a salad or side dish.

CRISPY NEW POTATOES WITH GOAT CHEESE

Yield: 4 to 6 servings

2 pounds small new potatoes

4 tablespoons butter

3 cloves of garlic, minced

1/2 teaspoon coarse sea salt

1 teaspoon cracked black pepper

1/3 cup goat cheese, crumbled

2 tablespoons fresh parsley, minced

2 tablespoons thyme leaves, minced

1 tablespoon fresh sage, minced

Clean the potatoes, but leave whole and do not peel. Place in a large pot and cover with water. Cover and bring to a boil; reduce the heat and simmer, covered, for about 20 minutes, or until potatoes are fork tender and cooked through. Drain off water and place pot with potatoes back on the burner.

Turn heat to low and heat potatoes, shaking pot occasionally, for a minute or so to evaporate any remaining moisture. Add the butter, garlic, salt and pepper and toss to coat. Turn heat to high and let the potatoes cook for about 2 minutes, stirring frequently, or until the skins begin to blister and turn golden. Once the skins are crispy, remove from heat and stir in the goat cheese and herbs. Serve immediately.

GRILLED POUND CAKE
WITH BLACKBERRIES AND LEMON CREAM

Grilled pound cake is one of my favorite desserts in the summer, and it is especially delicious with homemade ice cream. This more elegant variation uses a lemon cream that is divine if made with real whipped cream but still plenty tasty if you use the processed whipped topping, which has eclipsed the real thing in many a cowgirl's kitchen these days. Before you heat the grill, be sure to clean the grates very well and then lightly rub them with vegetable oil.

Yield: 6 servings

1 loaf-shaped pound cake, sliced about 1 1/2 inches thick

1 stick (1/2 cup) butter, softened

2 tablespoons honey

1 cup softly whipped cream, or whipped topping such as Cool Whip

1/2 cup lemon curd

3 cups whole blackberries

Vegetable oil for grilling

Lay the pound cake slices on a baking sheet. In a small bowl, thoroughly stir together the butter and honey and spread over both sides of the cake slices.

In a medium mixing bowl, fold together the whipped cream or topping and the lemon curd. Place in the freezer until ready to use.

Thoroughly clean grill grates and lightly rub with vegetable oil. Heat grill to medium. When grill is hot, place cake slices on the grill. Grill just until the cake develops grill marks, about 1 minute on each side.

Place a slice of cake on each plate. Top each slice with a generous spoonful of the lemon cream and 1/2 cup of the blackberries. Serve immediately.

CHAPTER 10
YELLOW ROSE GARDEN PARTY

MENU

Champagne Punch • Peach-Ginger Spritzer • Spicy Cheddar Cheese Straws • Gazpacho Shooters • Finger Sandwiches, Texas-Style • Purple-Hull Pea Salad • Blonde Brownies

Yellow roses symbolize friendship, good cheer and joy — and we all know the legendary Texas song. For me, roses also represent a reason to celebrate and an excuse to have a party. You see, I grew up in Tyler, Texas, a.k.a. the "Rose Capital of the World," and when roses bloom in May and October the city celebrates.

The party of the year takes place in October, when the town stages its annual Rose Festival: ladies lunching in their Sunday best; revelers lining the street for the parade; the young queen and her court extravagantly dressed in grand costumes, jeweled crowns and long trains.

I much prefer the more casual celebrations held in May. Spring is in full bloom, and everyone is ready to enjoy the beautiful weather before the summer heat wave begins. It's time to take advantage of the gardens; time to get together, for no good reason, and enjoy the great outdoors. And don't forget to stop and smell the roses!

Set the scene for your get-together with yellow roses everywhere, in containers large and small. For a more formal affair, antique urns, pitchers and vases make an elegant presentation, but for something fun and casual, I love the simplicity and contrast of yellow roses in blue Mason jars.

A few quick tips on arranging your rose bouquets: Remove all lower leaves, gather stems tightly and cut the stems to the height of the vase or jar. (Set the vessel next to the edge of the counter, hold the stems next to the counter and line up the blooms with the height you want them to be in the vessel; trim the stems even with the countertop.) A designer's rule of thumb when arranging with the same bloom and color is to use odd numbers of blooms. Use the roses alone or add stems of fresh herbs such as thyme, oregano or rosemary as filler.

Your table offers another great opportunity for mismatched china, silver and service pieces from flea markets, antique stores and Grandma's china cabinet. This menu is best served buffet-style, so stack an assortment of dessert or appetizer plates on the buffet table for grazing. For linens, I always like basic white tablecloths and napkins; for this party, a white lace overlay adds charm. If you don't have white cloth napkins, look at a craft or party store for paper napkins in the same shade as your yellow roses or for a color that contrasts with your service pieces or vases.

However you dress the tables, scatter them with yellow rose petals. If you have yellow roses in your garden, keep your eye on the blooms for a few days before the party and collect the petals from the blowsy ones just as they're about to fall. If you're buying from a florist, you can request that any unsold spent blooms be saved for you for a few days before your party. Try mounding most of the petals in the center of the tables, around your centerpieces, and scattering the petals more thinly toward the tables' perimeter. You want the petals to look as if they had just drifted there.

CHAMPAGNE PUNCH

My Grammy loved to throw parties, and this was her favorite punch. But don't let its sweetness fool you: With the addition of liqueur and brandy, it really packs a punch!

Use an inexpensive but drinkable cava or prosecco; make sure all the ingredients are well chilled, and mix the punch just before your guests arrive. Serve in a large punch bowl or in decorative glass pitchers, garnished with lemon slices and fresh raspberries.

Yield: 1 gallon

3 bottles sparkling wine

2 cans lemon-lime soda

1 1/2 cups brandy

3/4 cup raspberry liqueur

Juice from 8 lemons

1 cup powdered sugar, plus more to taste

Thin lemon slices and fresh raspberries, for garnish

Chill all ingredients. In a large punch bowl, combine sparkling wine, soda, brandy and liqueur.

Put the lemon juice in a separate bowl and stir in the sugar, mixing until sugar is dissolved. Add lemon mixture to punch bowl and stir to combine thoroughly.

Taste for sweetness and add more sugar, if desired.

PEACH-GINGER SPRITZER

Offer this lovely spritzer as a refreshing non-alcoholic alternative, served from decorative glass pitchers and garnished with fresh peach slices.

Yield: 7 cups

12-oz. can peach nectar, or 3 cups fresh peaches, peeled, pureed and strained through a fine-mesh sieve

2 tablespoons lemon juice

1 liter ginger ale

Ice, for serving

Peach slices, for garnish

In a large pitcher, combine peach nectar and lemon juice. Top with ginger ale. Stir to combine. Fill glasses with ice and pour in punch. Garnish rims with fresh peach slices.

SPICY CHEDDAR CHEESE STRAWS

When I was a child, my grandmother would make these every time the ladies were coming over for a round of bridge, gin rummy or evening cocktails. She always promised me the leftovers for myself but unfortunately they were always gone.

My grandmother made her cheese straws from a recipe by Helen Corbitt, the legendary Neiman Marcus food director who inspired generations of Texas cooks; this updated version has a bit more spice. I don't mind using prepared pie crust from the refrigerated section of the grocery store (NOT the frozen pie shells). If you prefer a flakier cheese straw, you could use puff pastry from the freezer section.

Serve these upright like bouquets in wine goblets or brandy snifters close to the bar and on side tables.

Yield: About 60 straws

1 cup shredded Cheddar cheese, divided
1 box refrigerated pie crusts (contains two rolled crusts)
Chipotle chile powder and salt, for sprinkling

Preheat oven to 400°. Grease an 18-by-13-inch baking sheet and set aside. Measure out 1/2 cup of cheese and divide it roughly into thirds; set the other 1/2 cup aside.

Flour a clean work surface thoroughly. Transfer one sheet of dough to the well-floured surface. (Keep other sheet of dough refrigerated.) Roll out the dough to 1/8-inch thickness, making it as nearly square as possible. Trim into a square with a sharp knife and discard trimmings. Mentally divide the dough in half horizontally and scatter a third of the cheese thinly over the half of the dough closest to you, leaving a narrow border bare around the three edges. Sprinkle the cheese lightly with chile powder and salt.

Fold top half of dough down over the bottom half and press all edges together. Fold this rectangle in half from left to right like a book.

Roll the folded dough out to make a 1/4-inch-thick rectangle. Sprinkle another third of the cheese and a light dusting of salt and chile powder on the bottom half as before; fold the top half down over the bottom half and then fold left to right.

Roll out dough again to 1/3-inch-thick. Repeat the sprinkling-and-folding steps above and roll out one last time, as thinly as possible. If there are some tears in the dough, especially around the seams and edges, that's OK. The final shape should be a long rectangle.

Repeat with other sheet of dough and remaining 1/2 cup cheese.

With a small sharp knife, cut the dough into strips 1/3-inch wide and then cut the strips into 6-inch sections. Grasp one end of each strip with each hand and twist to produce two twists in the strip. It should look like a loosely curled ribbon. Place twisted strips 1/2-inch apart on the greased baking sheet; they should fit on one sheet, but use another greased baking sheet if they don't. Bake for 6 to 8 minutes. Remove from oven, run a spatula under each straw to loosen it from the baking sheet and let the straws cool on the baking sheet.

These can be made a day in advance and stored unrefrigerated In a zip-top bag.

GAZPACHO SHOOTERS

This yummy summer soup is full of fresh flavors. It's a little spicy, very refreshing and perfectly balanced between sweet and savory. Serve it in shot glasses, cordial glasses or demitasse cups arranged on a mirror or large platter garnished with fresh mint leaves and yellow rosebuds.

Yield: 24 (2-oz.) servings

4 cups watermelon cubes (you'll need about a 3-pound watermelon)

2 large tomatoes, peeled, seeded and roughly chopped

1 cucumber, peeled, seeded and roughly chopped

2 Fresno peppers, cored, seeded and roughly chopped

1 cup cranberry juice

2 tablespoons white-wine vinegar

2 tablespoons lime juice

1/4 cup chopped fresh mint

2 tablespoons chopped fresh parsley

1/4 teaspoon salt

In a blender, combine all ingredients. Puree for about a minute, until fairly smooth. Transfer to a bowl, cover with plastic and refrigerate at least 1 hour, allowing mixture to chill completely and flavors to combine.

Just before serving, strain mixture through a fine-mesh sieve and discard any solids left in the sieve. Pour strained mixture into shot glasses or small serving cups.

Can be prepared one day in advance: Refrigerate unstrained; blend again briefly before serving and then strain.

FINGER SANDWICHES, TEXAS-STYLE

A garden party wouldn't be complete without finger sandwiches. But a cowgirl can't be serving dainty cucumber sandwiches; instead, these sandwiches have bold flavors guests will be excited to try. Wow them with bacon jam, spicy green chiles and everybody's favorite, pimento cheese.

Look for thin white sandwich bread and cut off the crusts before making sandwiches. After you've assembled the sandwiches, cut them into triangles, or use a biscuit or cookie cutter to cut into circles or other shapes. Stack each flavor separately on a tiered platter or cake plate.

BJLT (Bacon Jam, Lettuce and Tomato): Bacon jam can be found at specialty food stores, or you can make your own: Cook 1 pound bacon until just crisp; drain on a paper-towel-lined plate. Reserve

2 tablespoons of the bacon fat and discard the rest. While bacon is cooling, add to a slow cooker 1 thinly sliced sweet onion, 2 smashed cloves garlic, 1/2 cup water, 1/4 cup maple syrup, 1/4 cup brown sugar, 2 tablespoons balsamic vinegar, 2 tablespoons apple-cider vinegar and 1/2 teaspoon instant-coffee granules. When bacon is cool, roughly chop and add along with the reserved bacon fat. Cover cooker and cook on high for 2 hours, or until liquid has almost evaporated and mixture is syrupy. Let cool slightly; then transfer to a food processor and puree completely. Jam can be stored in a sealed container in the refrigerator for up to 1 week. Yield: 1 cup bacon jam, enough for 8 uncut sandwiches.

To make sandwiches, spread one side of bread thinly with bacon jam; add thinly sliced tomato and leafy lettuce.

Cream Cheese and Green Chiles: Combine 8 oz. softened cream cheese with 2 tablespoons chopped canned green chiles and 1 tablespoon prepared salsa. Yield: 1 cup, enough for 8 uncut sandwiches.

Homemade Pimento Cheese: In a mixing bowl, stir together 1/3 cup mayonnaise, 1/4 cup softened cream cheese, 2 tablespoons chopped pimentos, 1/2 teaspoon paprika and 1/4 teaspoon each salt and black pepper. When completely combined, mix in 2 cups shredded Cheddar cheese. For a creamier consistency, use an electric mixer to blend. Yield: About 1 1/2 cups, enough for 12 uncut sandwiches.

PURPLE-HULL PEA SALAD

Purple-hull peas are the tastier cousin of the black-eyed pea and are called such because of the bright-purple pods they grow in. This is a delicious salad any time of year, but it's extra-tasty during summer veggie season, when the peas, fresh corn and tomatoes are available at farm stands and markets. Serve it in an elegant glass or cut-crystal bowl and garnish with a little bouquet of fresh basil leaves.

Yield: 12 servings (7 cups)

2 cups shelled raw or frozen purple-hull peas

4 cups chicken or vegetable stock

1 tablespoon canola oil

2 cups frozen or fresh corn kernels (from about 3 medium ears of corn)

2 large tomatoes, seeded, cut into small dice

1/2 cucumber, seeded, cut into small dice

1/2 cup extra-virgin olive oil

1/3 cup apple-cider vinegar

1 tablespoon minced fresh parsley

1 tablespoon minced fresh basil

2 teaspoons Dijon mustard

2 teaspoons honey

1 teaspoon salt, or to taste

1/2 teaspoon black pepper, or to taste

Rinse peas with cold water in a colander. Pour stock into a large saucepan. Add peas and bring to a boil. Reduce heat and simmer uncovered about 20 minutes, until peas are tender. Drain peas and allow to cool in a large bowl.

Meanwhile, heat the canola oil in a sauté pan over high heat; add the corn kernels and sauté, stirring and shaking frequently, until golden and slightly charred. Allow to cool completely. Add corn to cooled peas; then add remaining ingredients and toss well.

Cover and refrigerate for at least 30 minutes before serving. Taste for seasoning before serving and add more salt and/or pepper if needed.

BLONDE BROWNIES

Looking through my mother's recipe box, I note that this card is hardly legible after all the times it's been used. These brownies were made for every occasion – birthdays, summer parties, housewarmings, weekend lake trips or long family road trips. I think your family will love them too. Serve them stacked on a cake stand dusted with powdered sugar.

Yield: About 35 1 1/2-inch-square brownies

2/3 cup butter, at room temperature, plus more for greasing pan

2 1/2 cups light-brown sugar

3 eggs

1 teaspoon vanilla

2 3/4 cups flour

2 1/2 teaspoons baking powder

1/2 teaspoon salt

6 oz. chocolate chips

3/4 cup chopped pecans

Grease a 13-by-9-inch baking pan. Preheat oven to 375°.

In a large bowl, using an electric mixer, cream the butter until soft; then add brown sugar gradually while continuing to cream. Beating constantly, add 1 egg at a time and then the vanilla.

In a separate bowl, sift together flour, baking powder and salt. Gradually beat dry ingredients, a little at a time, into the creamed butter mixture. Stir in the chocolate chips and the nuts.

Spread batter evenly in the greased pan and bake 35 to 45 minutes.

CHAPTER 11
WILD-GAME GATHERING: HOOVES, WINGS AND FINS

MENU

Shredded-Duck Crostini • Bacon-Wrapped Dove Kabobs • Caesar Salad With Pan-Fried Bass • Grilled Venison Backstrap With Mushroom-Berry Cream Sauce • Cheddar and Bacon Mashed-Potato Casserole • Chocolate Bourbon Pecan Pie

Learning to hunt and fish is a common rite of passage for Texas youngsters: Ask a cowgirl — even an urban cowgirl — and she'll probably tell you she's spent time on the deer lease or joined family or friends for fishing trips. She'll almost certainly tell you she's been tasked with cooking or eating whatever the hunters brought home.

And, when it comes to game, "tasked" can be the right word for the eating. It's the cooking that can make the difference between a grim dinner to be gamely endured or a special meal filled with the kind of deep flavors the supermarket can't provide. So what's a cowgirl to do with the catch of the day? Whether it's deer, duck or pheasant, here are a few universal tips:

• The flavor of the meat will depend on the age and sex of the animal, how it was processed and how long it took to harvest and chill the meat. Liquid and time are needed to pull blood out of the meat and muscle tissue before freezing or cooking; many hunters advise soaking the meat in milk or brining it in a mixture of water, salt and sugar. This is especially advisable for wild ducks and geese, though it's not typically necessary for small game birds like dove or quail.

• Game meat is typically very lean and becomes dry and gamey when overcooked. Brining, as mentioned above, adds moisture to the meat, as does cooking with a fatty ingredient like bacon. If you don't have the time or the inclination to brine, try marinating the meat for at least a couple of hours in the marinade of your choice. Most cuts of game benefit from low and slow cooking with liquid — braising or stewing. Many game recipes are bacon-wrapped or fried so as to tone down any gamey flavor that comes from the small amount of natural fat in the meat.

Hunters and fishermen have freezers filled with possibilities, and a wild-game dinner that features fowl, fish and hooves can be a fun evening. To add a patina of elegance, give your game dinner an English-country-house-meets-Texas-ranch theme. China patterns with hunting motifs have come back into fashion, and you can often find mismatched pieces of Spode Woodland, Arthur Court or American Wildlife in secondhand stores and at estate sales. All you need are a few pieces to accent the table.

Combine hunting-motif salad plates, for example, with plain white dinner plates. Instead of floral bouquets, fill pewter mugs with spires of fresh rosemary and decorative craft-store pheasant feathers. Duck decoys or small antlers make appropriate centerpieces when surrounded by greenery: ferns, pine and/or ivy. Wooden, pewter or dull-silver chargers, along with pewter service pieces, will accentuate the theme. Add crystal goblets or heavy glassware.

Appetizers can be served straight from a cutting board and the main dish from an ornate meat platter. Finish with dessert on themed dessert or salad plates, or saucers. Pass sweet tea and Texas beer in old silver pitchers. Choose a big red wine from one of the better Texas producers; if you have an antique (or antique-appearing) decanter, bring it out for the wine.

BASIC BRINING INSTRUCTIONS

A simple formula for brine is 8 cups water, 1/4 cup kosher salt and 2 tablespoons sugar. These amounts can be divided or multiplied according to the size of the meat you'll be brining. You'll need a vessel that's large enough to hold the meat and all the water but that still can fit in your refrigerator. Heat 2 cups of the water in the microwave until simmering; stir in the salt and the sugar until it is dissolved and set aside to cool. Meanwhile, place the meat in the brining vessel and pour 6 cups of cold water over it. When the water-salt mixture has cooled to room temperature, pour it in. The meat should be completely submerged. Cover and refrigerate up to 8 hours or overnight; then rinse the meat thoroughly and pat dry. The meat can now be frozen or cooked.

SHREDDED-DUCK CROSTINI

Wild ducks are quite different from the farm-raised ducks found in restaurants and grocery stores. The wild duck is very lean, tends to be tough and has a stronger flavor, which brining can ameliorate. Cooking the breast in a slow cooker keeps the meat from drying out and infuses other flavors and seasonings.

Yield: 16 crostini

4 duck breasts, skin removed, preferably brined according to instructions on Page 117

1/2 red onion, thinly sliced

1 cup orange juice

1/2 cup olive oil, divided

2 tablespoons coarse-grained mustard

1/2 teaspoon garlic salt

1 sourdough baguette

1 cup whipped cream cheese

2 tablespoons chopped canned green chiles

1/2 teaspoon black pepper

1/4 teaspoon salt

Place duck breasts and sliced onion in a slow cooker. In a measuring cup, combine the orange juice, 1/4 cup of the olive oil, the mustard and garlic salt. Pour into the slow cooker, cover and cook on high for 2 to 3 hours, or until meat is tender and easily shredded; pull meat into shreds with 2 forks. Meat can be held in the slow cooker for up to 1 hour on low.

When ready to assemble crostini, preheat oven to 325°. Slice baguette diagonally into 1/4-inch-thick slices, arrange on a baking sheet, brush baguette slices with remaining 1/4 cup olive oil and bake until lightly browned, about 5 minutes. Remove from the oven and let cool.

Meanwhile, in a small bowl, combine cream cheese, green chiles, pepper and salt. Spread the baguette slices with the cream-cheese mixture and top each with a spoonful of meat.

BACON-WRAPPED DOVE KABOBS

So many dove recipes call for a combination of bacon, jalapeno and cream cheese; when you bite into them, the dove meat is barely apparent. This recipe showcases the dove. You'll need 12 (6-inch) wooden or bamboo skewers (Asian markets sell these cheaply). Before you start the recipe, submerge the skewers in water (place a heavy object on top of them to keep them submerged) to soak while you're preparing the kabobs, so the skewers won't burn during grilling.

Yield: 12 kabobs

12 small new potatoes, unpeeled

1/2 teaspoon salt

1/2 teaspoon black pepper

12 slices bacon

6 whole dove breasts

1 red bell pepper

1/2 red onion

Place potatoes in a pan and cover with 2 inches of water. Bring to a boil and cook at a medium boil, uncovered, until barely fork-tender, about 10 minutes. Pour off water, leaving potatoes in pan. Add salt and pepper; toss to coat thoroughly. Set aside to cool to room temperature.

Cut each bacon slice in half. Debone the dove breasts, cut the two breast lobes apart and then cut each lobe into 2 evenly sized pieces, for a total of 4 pieces per breast. (It's important that the pieces be about the same size so the kabobs will cook evenly.) You'll end up with 24 pieces in all. Wrap each piece in bacon and set aside on a baking sheet.

Remove the stem, veins and seeds from the bell pepper and cut the pepper into 12 pieces about the same size as the pieces of dove. Cut the onion into 12 similar-size pieces.

Heat a grill or grill pan to high heat. Build your kabob by threading a piece of bell pepper onto the skewer, then a piece of dove breast (make sure the skewer goes through the bacon), a piece of onion, a piece of dove breast and a potato. Repeat with remaining skewers.

Cook skewers on the grill, turning every 3 minutes to cook all sides and adjusting heat if necessary. Remove from grill when bacon and dove meat are cooked through; be careful not to overcook the dove. Total grilling time should be about 10 to 12 minutes.

CAESAR SALAD WITH PAN-FRIED BASS

Yield: 8 servings

3 bass fillets, skin removed
Vegetable oil for frying
2 cups flour
1 teaspoon salt
1 teaspoon black pepper
1 teaspoon dry mustard
1 teaspoon paprika
4 cups coarsely chopped romaine lettuce
1 bottle Caesar dressing, divided
1 cup halved cherry tomatoes
1 cup croutons

1/2 cup shaved Parmesan cheese (a swivel-bladed peeler works well for this)

1 lemon, cut into 8 wedges, seeds removed

Cut the bass fillets into 1-by-3-inch strips. Heat 1 inch of vegetable oil in a skillet over high heat. In a shallow dish, thoroughly combine the flour, salt, pepper, dry mustard and paprika. When a pinch of the flour sizzles in the oil, it is ready.

Dredge the strips of bass in the flour mixture and carefully place them in the pan. Leave plenty of room between the strips to avoid crowding the skillet and cooling down the oil; cook in 2 batches if necessary. Fry on both sides until crisp and golden, about 5 minutes total. Monitor heat to prevent burning, and don't overcook the fish. Remove fish strips to a paper towel to drain and cool.

When ready to serve, add the romaine to a large serving bowl. Toss thoroughly with 1/4 to 1/2 cup of Caesar dressing: Start with the smaller amount and add more if necessary; you want just enough to lightly gloss the leaves but not so much that dressing pools in the bottom of the bowl. Top with the bass strips, tomatoes, croutons and cheese. Garnish with lemon wedges. Pour remaining dressing into a decorative bottle or cruet for passing at the table.

GRILLED VENISON BACKSTRAP WITH MUSHROOM-BERRY CREAM SAUCE

Chef Simon Webster owns Sabor a Pasion, an estate comprising a vineyard, B&B and restaurant, outside Palestine, Texas. One year the vineyard was being eaten up by deer, so he invited some hunters over for opening weekend of deer season. The result was this recipe.

Yield: 8 servings

2 teaspoons coarsely ground black pepper

1 teaspoon coarse sea salt

2 venison backstraps, whole, preferably brined as per instructions on Page 117

1 tablespoon olive oil

4 tablespoons butter, divided

2 cups sliced cremini mushrooms

1 cup dry red wine

1/4 cup cream

1 cup fresh or frozen mixed berries (blackberries, raspberries, blueberries)

2 teaspoons sugar

Combine the pepper and salt in a small bowl and rub each backstrap evenly with the seasoning. Heat a large grill pan or cast-iron skillet over high heat. Add oil, then 2 tablespoons of the butter.

Sear the backstraps 4 to 5 minutes on each side, until a deep-brown char develops and the backstrap is seared on all sides. Remove from heat and wrap in foil to rest until ready to serve.

In a sauté pan, melt remaining 2 tablespoons butter over medium-high heat. Add mushrooms and sauté, stirring them and shaking pan frequently, about 2 minutes, until browned. Add wine and let simmer for 1 minute. Stir in cream, berries and sugar. Bring to a boil and immediately remove from heat.

Unwrap meat and place on a platter; spoon sauce over the backstraps and serve.

CHEDDAR AND BACON MASHED-POTATO CASSEROLE

Yield: 8 servings

3 pounds Yukon gold potatoes, peeled and cut into chunks

4 whole cloves garlic, peeled

1 teaspoon salt

4 tablespoons butter

2 slices bacon

2 cups grated Cheddar cheese, divided

4 oz. cream cheese, softened

1/2 cup sour cream

1/4 cup chopped green onions

1 tablespoon olive oil

In a large saucepan, cover cubed potatoes and garlic with cold water and add salt. Bring to a boil over medium-high heat and cook at a medium boil until potatoes are fork-tender, about 20 minutes. Drain off water from pot and add butter to potatoes and garlic. Mash in the pot.

While potatoes are cooking, fry bacon in a skillet until crisp and remove to drain on paper towels before crumbling.

Preheat oven to 350°.

In a medium bowl, thoroughly stir together 1 cup of Cheddar cheese, the cream cheese and sour cream. Stir the mixture into the mashed potatoes and spoon potato mixture into a 9-by-13 baking dish, spreading evenly and smoothing top. Bake for 20 minutes or until heated through.

Meanwhile, in a small bowl, combine the remaining 1 cup Cheddar, green onions, crumbled bacon and olive oil. After potatoes have been in the oven 20 minutes, remove pan from oven, scatter the mixture over the top of the potatoes and return to oven to cook for an additional 10 minutes, until topping is melted and bubbly.

CHOCOLATE BOURBON PECAN PIE BARS

Yield: 12 servings

CRUST

2/3 cup sugar
1/2 cup butter, melted
1 teaspoon vanilla
1 1/2 cups flour

TOPPING

3 eggs, beaten
1 cup light corn syrup
3/4 cup sugar
2 tablespoons melted butter
2 tablespoons bourbon
2 teaspoons vanilla
1/4 teaspoon salt
1 cup chopped pecans
1/4 cup semi-sweet chocolate chips

CRUST

Preheat oven to 350°. Grease a 9-by-13-inch pan with cooking spray.
In a large mixing bowl, stir together sugar, butter and vanilla; gradually
stir in flour. Pat crust mixture evenly into the bottom of the pan.
Bake for 15 to 17 minutes, until edges are light brown. Cool to room
temperature before topping.

TOPPING

In large mixing bowl, combine eggs, corn syrup, sugar, butter, bourbon,
vanilla and salt. Beat on low with an electric mixer for 1 minute. Stir in
the pecans and chocolate chips.

ASSEMBLY

Pour filling evenly into cooled crust. Bake at 350° for 25 minutes, or
until filling is set. Using a spatula, loosen edges from the side of the pan
while still warm. Let cool for 1 hour and then cut into 2-inch squares.

CHAPTER 12
CATTLEMAN'S COCKTAIL PARTY

MENU

Dirty Jalapeño Martinis • Texas Cowgirl Cocktails • Tiny Tostadas With Spicy Chicken Salad • Broiled Jalapeño Poppers • Crab-Stuffed Avocados • Bruschetta of Rare Beef With Blue-Cheese Horseradish and Basil Gremolata • Neiman Marcus Cake Bars • Cow Pie Cookies

Growing up in Texas during the late '70s and early '80s was a young cowgirl's dream. Dolly Parton, Loretta Lynn and Barbara Mandrell were headlining the Houston Livestock Show & Rodeo. *Dallas* was everyone's favorite Friday night TV show; the popularity of its characters, fashion, iconography and setting had made longhorns and Wrangler jeans a worldwide phenomenon.

And, in the real Dallas, the Cattle Baron's Ball was making society headlines as the quintessential Texas celebration. It was a hot ticket from its beginning, as a lavish ranch barbecue to benefit the American Cancer Society in 1974, when Jacque Wynne and Patti Hunt brought in Johnny Cash and had custom Stetsons made for the higher-donating gentlemen. This annual society shindig, which has spawned spinoffs throughout the state and beyond, is the quintessential Texas celebration, raising millions for cancer research and family support — a crowning example of Texas food, fashion, music and style.

I remember watching my parents get ready for the Cattle Baron's gala and seeing all the pictures in the newspaper after the party. I loved hearing what everyone was wearing and wanted to know all about all the fanciful cowboy canapés that were served.

But really, as Texans, this kind of upscale ranch-style entertaining is something we do more than once a year. Fund-raisers, client dinners and special occasions happen all the time, and sometimes we just need an excuse to starch the Sunday Wranglers and shine up our coolest pair of python Luccheses or hand-tooled M.L. Leddy's. That blend of fancy and sophisticated with fun and relaxed is a trademark of parties thrown by Texas cowgirls.

This party is my homage to Texas-style entertaining, inspired by all the ideals and stereotypes we know and love about the Lone Star State. For me, these recipes represent classic Texas hors d'oeuvre: Some have a modern twist, and others really should stay exactly the same as they were 30 years ago.

For this soirée, pull out all the stops. Set up a buffet table accented with crystal vases filled with elegant stems: tulips, irises, vividly colored lilies, birds of paradise, tall alliums. Raid the china cabinet for silver and crystal; don't be afraid to mix traditional with modern. Cover your buffet table with white or black linens; use boxes or cake stands of differing heights under the linens to elevate some of the platters.

Arrange the food on elegant white platters or silver trays lined with glass plates; garnish your platters with accenting ingredients. For the Tiny Tostadas, you might top each cup with a cilantro leaf, dust chili powder around the edges of the platter (a fine sieve is a good tool for this) and grate a drift of lime zest over the top. Fresh herbs such as rosemary, sage and mint always add appeal when tucked in abundance onto a plate, and fig or grape leaves make striking liners for platters or cheese boards. To dress up the Neiman Marcus Cake Bars, you've got lots of options: Top each with a strawberry slice and maybe a tiny mint leaf. Or center a roasted pecan half atop each, or use a baking stencil to create a design on each bar with sieved powdered sugar or cocoa (ditto for the Cow Pie Cookies).

Serve the cocktails in classic martini glasses and tall, skinny highball glasses, with appropriate garnishes. Have a few already made and arranged on a tray for when guests arrive. Ideally, you should have someone who can man the bar and prepare the cocktails, which are best shaken rather than stirred. If you're short-handed, though, simply multiply the cocktail recipes and prepare pitchers of each libation.

DIRTY JALAPEÑO MARTINIS

Adding a hint of heat is just as good in a cocktail as it is in food.

Yield: 2 cocktails

4 oz. vodka

2 teaspoons pickled jalapeño juice (from jar of pickled jalapeños)

1 to 2 teaspoons olive brine from jar

1 teaspoon dry vermouth

Jalapeño-stuffed olives, for garnish

Fill a cocktail shaker with ice. Add vodka, jalapeño juice, olive brine and vermouth. Cover and shake vigorously for 5 to 10 seconds. Pour into chilled martini glasses. Garnish with olives.

TEXAS COWGIRL COCKTAILS

This quintessential Texas cowgirl cocktail contains flavors from some of the Lone Star State's favorite fruits. It also needs tequila – the liquor of the desert Southwest. With three different spirits, this drink packs a punch, but that's part of a cowgirl's qualities – strong, sweet, colorful and refreshing.

Yield: 2 cocktails

3 oz. peach schnapps

2 oz. triple sec orange liqueur

2 oz. tequila

1 cup fresh-squeezed grapefruit juice

Fresh peach slices, for garnish

Mint sprigs, for garnish

Fill a cocktail shaker with ice. Add the schnapps, triple sec and tequila. Cover and shake vigorously for 5 to 10 seconds. Pour into ice-filled highball glasses. Top with grapefruit juice and garnish each with peach slices and a sprig of mint.

TINY TOSTADAS WITH SPICY CHICKEN SALAD

Purchase the cup-shaped tortilla chips commonly marketed as "scoops." A bag will contain more "scoops" than you need, but many will be broken. You can make the chipotle chicken salad up to a day in advance; however, to prevent browning, the avocado mixture must be made no more than 2 hours before serving time. To ensure a crispy bite, wait until just before guests arrive to assemble the tostadas.

Yield: about 20 mini-tostadas

2 soft avocados

1/4 cup sour cream

3 tablespoons lime juice

1/2 teaspoon black pepper

1/4 teaspoon salt

1/4 cup mayonnaise

1 to 2 canned chipotle peppers, chopped

2 grilled chicken breasts, shredded

10-oz. bag tortilla-chip cups, or "scoops"

Chile powder, for dusting

Zest of 1 lime

Halve and seed avocados, scoop out flesh into a medium bowl. Add sour cream, lime juice, pepper and salt; mash together until smooth and well-blended. Set aside.

In a medium bowl, combine the mayonnaise and chopped chipotle. Stir in shredded chicken. Taste for seasoning and add salt and pepper if needed.

Pick out about 20 of the most perfect tortilla-chip cups. Divide the avocado mixture among them; then top each with a dab of the chicken salad. Lightly dust with chili powder and lime zest. Serve immediately.

BROILED JALAPEÑO POPPERS

Red jalapeños, if you can find them, make a striking presentation, either by themselves or interspersed with the green ones. The jalapeños can be assembled a day in advance and refrigerated; bring to room temperature for 2 hours before broiling.

Yield: 12 canapés

6 large jalapeños

2 oz. cream cheese, room temperature

2 oz. soft goat cheese, room temperature

1/2 cup grated sharp Cheddar

1/2 teaspoon black pepper

1/4 teaspoon salt

Preheat broiler to 450°. Halve and seed each jalapeño.

In a bowl, thoroughly blend together cream cheese and goat cheese; blend in grated Cheddar, pepper and salt. Using a small spoon, fill each jalapeño half with about 1 tablespoon cheese mixture.

Place peppers on a parchment-lined baking sheet and broil until cheese is browned and bubbling, about 5 to 10 minutes. Watch closely and rotate baking sheet for even cooking.

CRAB-STUFFED AVOCADOS

Serving avocados at a cocktail party can be tricky because of their tendency to darken after being cut, but after testing many recipes I've learned that avocados will stay bright green for at least a couple of hours after being cut. Rubbing lemon juice on the exposed areas of the avocado or placing it in ice water helps keep oxidation at bay. Still, it's best to put these together as close to serving time as possible, though you can make the crab salad the morning of your event.

Yield: 12 servings

1/2 cup lemon juice, divided

2 tablespoons mayonnaise

1 tablespoon olive oil

1/2 teaspoon black pepper

1/4 teaspoon salt

1 pound fresh lump crabmeat

6 small ripe avocados

Red leaf lettuce, for garnish

1/4 cup chopped fresh Italian parsley

Grated zest of 1 lemon

In a medium bowl, whisk 1/4 cup of the lemon juice together with the mayonnaise, olive oil, pepper and salt. Gently fold in the crabmeat just to distribute, being very careful to not break up or crush the meat too much. Refrigerate until ready to serve.

Cut avocados in half, remove seed and use a large spoon to remove the avocado halves from the skin. Use a tablespoon to make each seed hole a bit larger, about an inch in diameter. Using a basting brush, brush the remaining 1/4 cup lemon juice over the top and exterior flesh of the avocado. Spoon the crab salad into the avocados. Arrange lettuce leaves on a platter and place the avocado halves atop the lettuce (slice a tiny bit horizontally off the bottom of the avocado halves if necessary to make them sit upright). Garnish with a scattering of chopped parsley and lemon zest.

BRUSCHETTA OF RARE BEEF WITH BLUE-CHEESE HORSERADISH AND BASIL GREMOLATA

Except for the gremolata, each element can be cooked or prepared up to 8 hours before service. For the beef, cook, slice and refrigerate; bring to room temperature for 1 hour before assembling. The bread can be toasted in advance and stored in a zip-top bag at room temperature (place toast in the bag before it cools). Refrigerate the horseradish spread, allowing 1 hour to come to room temperature. Assemble the bruschetta 30 minutes before guests arrive.

Yield: about 15 bruschetta

1 pound beef tenderloin

2 tablespoons steak seasoning

2 tablespoons vegetable oil

1 baguette, sliced into 1/2-inch-thick slices

1/4 cup olive oil

1/4 cup sour cream

2 tablespoons crumbled blue cheese

1 tablespoon prepared horseradish

1 teaspoon dry mustard

1/4 cup cream

15 basil leaves

Zest of 2 lemons

3 large cloves garlic

1/4 teaspoon coarse sea salt

1/2 teaspoon coarse black pepper

Extra-virgin olive oil, for garnish

Place the beef on a plate and rub the steak seasoning into the meat. Heat a grill pan to high and add the vegetable oil. When the oil begins to smoke, add the beef and sear on all sides for 2 to 3 minutes per side. Remove to a plate and let the meat rest for 15 minutes.

Preheat oven to 400°. Brush the baguette slices with olive oil on both sides and place on a baking sheet; bake for about 5 minutes. Turn the bread and bake for an additional couple of minutes, or until lightly toasted and golden. Set aside to cool.

In a medium bowl, combine the sour cream, blue cheese, horseradish and dry mustard, mashing all together with the back of a spoon until smooth and well-distributed. Stir in the cream until blended.

Spread a couple of teaspoons of the blue-cheese mixture onto each baguette slice, dividing it equally.

Make the basil gremolata: Stack the basil leaves and roll tightly. Slice into ribbons and then chop finely. Place the basil in a bowl with the lemon zest. Lay the garlic cloves flat on a cutting board and crush with the back of a chef's knife; discard outer peel. Sprinkle cloves with salt and pepper and chop finely. Add to the bowl with the basil and lemon zest and toss together.

Using a very sharp knife, slice the seared beef very thinly, no thicker than 1/8 inch. Divide the beef slices atop the baguette slices, folding to fit. Arrange the bruschetta on a serving platter. Lightly drizzle the extra-virgin olive oil over the bruschetta and around the platter, and sprinkle with the basil gremolata.

NEIMAN MARCUS CAKE BARS

This butter cake was often on the menu at my sorority house at Texas A&M. It was probably why we all gained 10 pounds after moving into the house. After doing some research, I could find no evidence this recipe actually came from the Neiman Marcus department store. My best guess is the name comes from its rich, decadent flavor that makes it an irresistible indulgence.

Yield: 30 bars

CAKE

2 eggs
1/2 cup melted butter (1 stick)
1 cup chopped pecans
18.25-oz. box yellow cake mix

GLAZE

2 eggs
8-oz. package cream cheese, room temperature
1 teaspoon almond extract
3 1/2 cups powdered sugar, plus more for dusting

CAKE

Preheat oven to 350°. In a mixing bowl, combine the 2 eggs, melted butter, chopped pecans and cake mix. Stir with a spatula until all ingredients are completely incorporated. Lightly grease a 9-by-13 baking pan with cooking spray or butter and spread the batter evenly in the pan. Set aside.

GLAZE

With an electric mixer, combine the 2 eggs, cream cheese and almond extract. With mixer on, gradually add powdered sugar until blended. Pour this mixture on top of the cake mixture. Bake at 350° for 10 minutes; then turn oven to 325° and bake for 25 to 30 more minutes, using a toothpick inserted into the center of the cake as a tester to make sure cake is cooked. Remove from oven and let cool in the pan.

When cake has cooled, run a knife around the edges to loosen; then cut into 30 bars about 2 inches square. Dust with additional powdered sugar.

COW PIE COOKIES

Yield: 3 to 4 dozen cookies

1/2 cup Crisco shortening, room temperature

1/2 cup (1 stick) butter, room temperature

1 cup packed light-brown sugar

1 cup granulated sugar

2 eggs

1 teaspoon vanilla

1 teaspoon baking soda

1 teaspoon baking powder

2 cups flour

1/2 cup instant oats

1 cup crushed cornflakes

1/2 cup sweetened coconut flakes

1/2 cup chopped pecans

1 cup semi-sweet chocolate chips

Preheat oven to 350°. In a large bowl, using an electric mixer, cream together the Crisco, butter and sugars. Continuing to beat, add eggs one at a time; then vanilla, baking soda, baking powder and flour.

With a spatula or large spoon, gently fold in the oats, cornflakes, coconut, pecans and chocolate chips.

Grease 2 cookie sheets and drop dough by teaspoonfuls 1/2-inch apart on the sheets. Bake for 8 to 10 minutes. Let cool slightly and remove with a spatula to a cooling rack.

INDEXES

RECIPE INDEX

APPETIZERS AND CANAPÉS

BEVERAGES

Peach-Ginger Spritzer, 107
Peach Iced Tea, 96
Peach Mojitos, 86
Strawberry Lemonade, 52
Strawberry-Lime Gin and Tonic, 96
Strawberry-Melon Coolers, 87
Sweet Mint Iced Tea, 38
Texas Cowgirl Cocktails, 129
Texas Summer Shandy, 26
Watermelon-Lime Rickey, 52

BREADS

Banana Bread Trifle, 47
Blueberry Blue-Corn Muffins, 17
Chuckwagon Almond Croissants, 70
Skillet Honey Cornbread, 63
Spicy Cheddar Cheese Straws, 107
Sweet-Potato Bread, 45

BREAKFAST AND BRUNCH

Blueberry Blue-Corn Muffins, 17
Baked Mexican Frittata With Hash-Brown Crust, 18
Chilaquiles Rojo, 69
Chuckwagon Almond Croissants, 70
Wildflower Honey Granola Parfait, 20

DESSERTS

Banana Bread Trifle, 47
Blonde Brownies, 113
Chocolate Bourbon Pecan Pie Bars, 124
Cow Pie Cookies, 136
Dark-Chocolate Sheet Cake, 48
Grilled Pound Cake With Blackberries and Lemon Cream, 102

Neiman Marcus Cake Bars, 135
Pecan Pie Shortbread Cookies, 124
Red, White and Blue Pie, 59
Sopapilla Cheesecake Cookies, 82
Strawberry Chess Squares, 21
Tropical Dump Cake, 67

MAIN ENTREES

Bourbon-Braised Short Ribs, 30
Classic Tex-Mex Beef & Cheese Enchiladas, 77
Cowgirl Stew, 65
Grilled Butterflied Chicken, 28
Grilled Venison Backstrap With Mushroom-Berry Cream Sauce, 121
King Ranch Chicken, 40
Rosemary-Grilled Lamb Chops With Fresh Mint Sauce, 98
Slow Cooker Sunday Ham, 44
Texas Gulf Coast Crab Boil, 92
Tex-Mex Fish & Chips, 55

SALADS

Caesar Salad With Pan-Fried Bass, 120
Garden-Fresh Guacamole, 75
Grilled Green-Tomato Caprese Salad, 54
Mom's Potato Salad, 31
Purple-Hull Pea Salad, 112
Sweet and Crunchy Coleslaw, 33
Three-Bean Salad, 39

SANDWICHES /CROSTINI/BRUSCHETTA

Bruschetta of Rare Beef With Blue-Cheese Horseradish and Basil
Gremolata, 133
Finger Sandwiches, Texas-Style, 110

Bacon Jam, Lettuce and Tomato, 110
Cream Cheese and Green Chile, 111
Homemade Pimento Cheese, 111
Fried-Oyster Sliders With Spicy Lime Mayonnaise, 89
Shredded-Duck Crostini, 117

SIDE DISHES

SOUPS

CATEGORY INDEX

CAKES

CASSEROLES

Cheddar and Bacon Mashed-Potato Casserole, 123
Classic Tex-Mex Beef & Cheese Enchiladas, 77
Cheesy Pineapple Casserole, 41
King Ranch Chicken, 40

COOKIES AND BARS

Blonde Brownies, 113
Cow Pie Cookies, 136
Neiman Marcus Cake Bars, 135
Pecan Pie Shortbread Cookies, 34
Sopapilla Cheesecake Cookies, 82
Strawberry Chess Squares, 21

FISH (see SEAFOOD)

FOWL

Chicken
 Grilled Butterflied Chicken, 28
 King Ranch Chicken, 40
 Tiny Tostadas With Spicy Chicken Salad, 129
Dove
 Bacon-Wrapped Dove Kabobs, 119
Duck
 Shredded-Duck Crostini, 117

MEATS

Beef
 Bourbon-Braised Short Ribs, 30
 Bruschetta of Rare Beef With Blue-Cheese Horseradish and Basil
Gremolata, 133
 Cowgirl Stew, 65

Lamb
  Rosemary-Grilled Lamb Chops With Fresh Mint Sauce, 98
Pork
  Big Bold BBQ Layered Dip, 26
  Slow Cooker Sunday Ham, 44
Venison
  Grilled Venison Backstrap With Mushroom-Berry Cream Sauce, 121

PIES
  Chocolate Bourbon Pecan Pie, 124
  Red, White and Blue Pie, 59

SEAFOOD
  Caesar Salad With Pan-Fried Bass, 120
  Corn and Crab-Claw Fritters, 133
  Crab-Stuffed Avocados, 65
  Crawfish-and-Cornbread-Stuffed Mushrooms, 87
  Fried-Oyster Sliders With Spicy Lime Mayonnaise, 89
  Shrimp Tostadas With Grapefruit Salsa, 90
  Texas Gulf Coast Crab Boil, 92
  Tex-Mex Fish & Chips, 55

SALSAS AND RELISHES
  Garden-Fresh Guacamole, 75
  Heirloom Tomato Salsa, 97
  Watermelon Salsa, 76

SLOW COOKER DISHES
  Bacon Jam, 111
  Big Bold BBQ Layered Dip, 26
  Shredded-Duck Crostini, 117
  Slow Cooker Sunday Ham, 44

THE AUTHOR

When Christine Gardner isn't cooking, she's looking after two horses, three longhorns and an ever-changing menagerie of animals on 25 acres in the Piney Woods of East Texas. Raised as a "city cowgirl" in Dallas, Tyler and Houston, she's in the kitchen writing and testing recipes most days and spends her evenings teaching cooking classes, catering events and hosting Texas-size celebrations that highlight her cowgirl style. Classically trained with French technique from Le Cordon Bleu, she apprenticed with a chef in Italy but has never forsaken her Texas roots. Her first cookbook, *Favorite Flavor*, was released in 2013, and she hosts a cooking show on KYTX-CBS19 in Tyler.